Intercultural
Communicative Language
Teaching and TCSOL

跨文化交际
与国际汉语教学

英汉对照

（英）迈克尔·拜拉姆（Michael Byram） 著
和静 赵媛 译

外语教学与研究出版社
FOREIGN LANGUAGE TEACHING AND RESEARCH PRESS
北京 BEIJING

图书在版编目（CIP）数据

跨文化交际与国际汉语教学：英汉对照 ／（英）迈克尔·拜拉姆（Michael Byram）著；和静，赵媛译 . -- 北京：外语教学与研究出版社，2017.5（2019.5 重印）
（世界汉语教学学会名师讲座系列）
ISBN 978-7-5135-9155-3

Ⅰ.①跨… Ⅱ.①迈… ②和… ③赵… Ⅲ.①文化交流 - 研究 - 英、汉②汉语 - 对外汉语教学 - 教学研究 - 英、汉 Ⅳ.①G115②H195.3

中国版本图书馆 CIP 数据核字（2017）第 137670 号

出 版 人　蔡剑峰
责任编辑　张立萍
装帧设计　姚 军
图片摄影　姚 军
出版发行　外语教学与研究出版社
社　　址　北京市西三环北路 19 号（100089）
网　　址　http://www.fltrp.com
印　　刷　北京虎彩文化传播有限公司
开　　本　787×1092 1/16
印　　张　11
版　　次　2017 年 7 月第 1 版 2019 年 5 月第 3 次印刷
书　　号　ISBN 978-7-5135-9155-3
定　　价　45.00 元

购书咨询：（010）88819926　电子邮箱：club@fltrp.com
外研书店：https://waiyants.tmall.com
凡印刷、装订质量问题，请联系我社印制部
联系电话：（010）61207896　电子邮箱：zhijian@fltrp.com
凡侵权、盗版书籍线索，请联系我社法律事务部
举报电话：（010）88817519　电子邮箱：banquan@fltrp.com
物料号：291550001

记载人类文明
沟通世界文化
www.fltrp.com

出版说明
Publisher's Note

  随着"汉语热"的不断升温，汉语教学和汉语应用的全球化趋势日益明显。截至 2016 年 12 月 31 日，全球已有 140 个国家和地区建立了 512 所孔子学院和 1073 个孔子课堂。然而，在国际汉语教学快速发展的同时，我们也面临着许多问题和挑战。例如，国际汉语教师人数相对不足，师资队伍建设有待进一步加强；本土化教材开发亟待新的突破；急需探索高效可行的教学方法等。在诸多挑战之中，教学方法的选择又成为重中之重，直接决定了教学的质量与效果。在这样的背景下，跨文化交际语言教学作为国际新兴的教学模式，将语言教学与文化教学相结合，力图培养具有国际视野和开放心态的语言学习者，在信息全球化的 21 世纪受到了二语习得教师的普遍青睐。

  针对国内和国际教学的现状，世界汉语教学学会于 2016 年夏季特别举办了"跨文化交际与国际汉语教育高级讲习班"。此次讲习班特别邀请到英国杜伦大学教育学荣休教授 Michael Byram。这是 Michael Byram 教授首次为国际汉语教师作讲座。他用大量语言教学实例深入浅出地阐释了跨文化交际语言教学的基本概念和要素，介绍了跨文化交际语境下的课程与课程规划方法，探究了教师与学生在教与学过程中的评价与评估问题，并提出了语言教学中的人文主义与教育目标——用于提高学习者对自身文化及他者文化的批判性理解。很多教师和研究者慕名而来，并就汉语教学中的问题与 Michael Byram 教授进行了积极的互动。

Michael Byram 教授的讲座非常具有启发性、实践性和学术价值。应许多参会教师的要求，在征得了 Michael Byram 教授同意之后，外研社国际汉语出版中心以 Michael Byram 教授的四场讲座内容为素材，精心推出了《跨文化交际与国际汉语教学》一书。本书主要有以下特点：

1. 呈现方式：本书打破传统学术书籍的纯英文版或纯中文版呈现方式，中英文并排的形式使本书便携、易懂，更适合国际汉语教师和学生深入理解跨文化语言教学模式新理念，节省查阅工具书的时间，提高研读效率。

2. 选材来源：英文以 Michael Byram 教授的四场讲座内容为原材料，还囊括了受邀嘉宾——北京语言大学外国语学院王丽虹副教授的讲座内容。作为 Michael Byram 教授的博士生，她在此系列讲座中就国际汉语教材的转型做了深入浅出的分析，以生动的汉语教学实例引起了在座学者的共鸣。考虑到不偏离其语言风格和讲座的整体流畅性，全稿英文在修订过程中保留了个别口语片段表达等。中文主要来自现场的同声传译材料，同传译员为北京外国语大学孔子学院工作处和静副处长和高级翻译学院赵媛老师。本书编辑修改了口译材料中的一些口误、重复、语法等问题，将材料进行了一定程度的语言书面化加工，整体上内容取材于现场讲座，所以中文和英文都偏向口语的语言风格，亲切易懂。

3. 立体性阅读体验：读者可通过扫描封面二维码或登录封面网址获取现场讲座视频，深入感受现场讲座及交流气氛，加深对本书内容的理解。

最后，希望本书可以为广大国际汉语教师及研究生、第二语言教学研究者和对国际汉语教学感兴趣的人士提供帮助，帮助他们深入理解跨文化交际语言教学研究领域的新理念，并最终应用到教学实践中。

外语教学与研究出版社
国际汉语出版中心

目录
Contents

引　言

　　在本次"跨文化交际与国际汉语教育高级讲习班"上，我将给大家做四场讲座。首先我会给大家做一个概述，这四场讲座的内容是关于语言教学中的跨文化视角的。在第一场讲座开始之前，我希望大家思考一下"跨文化"的含义。

　　比如，刚才主持人介绍我是"Michael Byram 教授"，有些人，包括在座的一位，会叫我"Mike"，所以，我们彼此称呼的方式，无论你是叫我的全名、头衔，还是简称 Mike，都是具有文化意义的。我有很多学生来自亚洲国家——中国、韩国、日本、新加坡。我总是跟他们说"叫我 Mike"，但是很多人不喜欢叫我 Mike，有些人还是叫我"Mike 教授"。所以，我们已经涉及跨文化的问题了。我们彼此交谈的方式里面就存在跨文化问题。

　　那应该怎么称呼呢？答案可以是多种多样的。你可以遵循欧洲语言的特点，"入乡随俗"。或者说，如果我来到中国，来到北京，我就应该用当地人的称呼方式。大家怎么称呼我，我也应该怎么称呼大家。如果我希望成为中国人，或按照中国人的习惯做事，这是一种方式。还有另外一种可能，大家可能会直接叫我 Mike，我经常这么跟学生说，让他们直接叫我 Mike，但是如果我这么说，就是把我所在大学的称呼方式强加给了大家。我特意强调"我所在大学"而不是"西方"，因为在"西方"，称呼方式也是多种多样的，但在我的大学和我所在的系，直呼名字 Mike，是很正常的事情。然而，如果我说"你必须叫我 Mike"，实际上就是把我习惯的方式强加给了大家，有人可能称之为"文化帝国主义"。所以我们可能需要找到第三种方法，即"跨文化的文化"，既不是中式的，也不是英式的，

Introduction

At this "Intercultural Communicative Language Teaching and International Chinese Language Education Senior Workshop", I'm going to be with you to give four lectures. And I'm first of all going to give an overview of the four lectures, which are about intercultural matters in language teaching. Before I begin my first lecture, I want you to think about what 'intercultural' means.

For example, I have been just introduced as 'Professor Michael Byram'. Some people including one person here in the room would simply call me 'Mike'. So the ways in which we talk to each other, whether we use my full name and my title or use the short form 'Mike', is already a matter of culture. I've had many students from Asia – from China, from South Korea, from Japan, from Singapore – and I always say to them 'call me Mike', but many of them don't like to call me 'Mike'. So some of them say 'Professor Mike'. So we have already a kind of intercultural problem, something that already begins with how we talk to each other.

What's the answer? There are many possible answers to a little problem like this. One can do as we say in European languages, 'When in Rome, do as the Romans'. In other words, here in China, in Beijing, I should use the same approach to address you as you use in addressing me. That's one way where I would try to become a Chinese or rather follow the Chinese way of doing things. Another possibility would be for you to call me 'Mike' as I often said to my students, but that might be me imposing upon you my way of doing things in my university. I say deliberately 'my university' and not 'the West'. Because in 'the West', things are very varied, but in my university and in my department of my university, using first names like 'Mike' is normal. However, if I say 'you must call me Mike', then that is me imposing upon you my way of doing things, and one might call that 'cultural imperialism'. So maybe we have to find a third possibility,

而是介于两者之间的。这种"跨文化的文化"正是本次系列讲座中一个重要的概念。

An intercultural workshop...

Preliminary remarks

- introductions - names, titles, etc. within 'the West'
  - AND HERE [in this workshop]?
- Possible answers:
  - 'When in Rome, do as the Romans'?? = I (try to) become a Chinese
  - OR 'follow the teacher' = cultural imperialism
  - OR an intercultural culture

概述

现在回到讲座概述。首先,我会谈到跨文化交际语言教学(ICLT)中的一些基本问题,寻找阐述文化这一概念的例子:"文化到底是什么意思?"其次,我会谈一下课程和课程规划的问题。第三部分是评估与评价。最后是跨文化交际语言教学(ICLT)中的批判性思维和人文主义目标。

Titles and content

1 Fundamental issues in intercultural communicative language teaching (ICLT)
       - concepts (e.g. 'culture')
2 Curriculum and lesson planning
3 Assessment and evaluation
4 Critical thinking and the humanistic purposes of ICLT - the way forward

---

我的目的是给大家讲一些重要的观念,以及它们为什么重要。之后我会为大家介绍一位嘉宾,在其帮助下我会给大家展示一些例子,希望能够通过例子帮助你们去理解和应用这些观念。

which is an 'intercultural culture' where we find something which is not Chinese, not English, but somewhere in between. This idea of 'intercultural culture' is an idea that is going to be important in my lectures.

Overview

I can now come to my overview. To begin with, I'll talk about some fundamental issues in intercultural communicative language teaching (ICLT), looking for examples at the concept of culture: 'What do we mean by culture?' Then, I'll talk about curriculum and lesson planning. Thirdly, I will talk about assessment and evaluation, and finally about critical thinking and the humanistic purposes of ICLT.

My purpose is to explain some ideas, and why I think they are important. I'm going to show you some examples, with the help of someone I will introduce later, and I hope to help you to understand and apply those ideas through the examples.

What is my aim?

- To explain some ideas and why they are important
- To show some examples
- To help you understand and apply ideas

Where are we going? What is our ultimate destination over the course of these lectures? I want to explain this by referring to 'College English' with which you are familiar. Although you are teachers of Chinese, I think we can refer to this document about teaching English in China because it is a very good statement about language teaching of any kind, anywhere. It says in the *College English Teaching Syllabus* that English or Chinese or French or any foreign language is part of humanity education, liberal arts education. It has two purposes: instrumental and humanistic.

　　我要说的是什么？这一系列讲座的终极目标是什么呢？我想通过"大学英语"这个你们所熟悉的概念来解释一下。虽然你们都是汉语教师，但我想在中国教英语也一样适用，实际上这也是一个适用于任何地方的任何语言教学的指南。《大学英语教学大纲》中写到，英语、汉语、法语或者其他外语，实际上都是人文教育的一部分，都属于文科，其本身既具有工具性，也具有人文性。

　　这就预示了无论是在中国还是在其他国家，所有的语言教学，特别是跨文化语言教学，都有十分明确的跨文化教育目标，即帮助学生了解不同的思维方式、不同的价值观，以及本国（对大家而言是中国）与其他国家之间的差异和相似之处。换句话说，就是要培养学生的跨文化交际意识，要让他们知道如何去理解，同时提高学生的社会、语言和跨文化交际能力。这是针对大学英语教学的，但也适用于其他外语的教学。该方法综合了两个目的：一个是在语言教学中占主导的工具性目的，即语言是用于交流的；一个是尚未得到充分认可的人文性目的，即通过语言教学，帮助语言学习者了解他人、了解自己。

This suggests that in all language teaching – and in my view especially in intercultural communicative language teaching – in China as elsewhere, there are clear aims of intercultural education: to understand other ways of thinking, other values, and the differences and similarities between our country (China in your case) and other countries. This means in other words, to cultivate students' intercultural awareness, how they understand things, and to improve their social, linguistic and intercultural communication abilities. This is clearly stated for College English, and it is a good statement about any foreign language teaching. This approach combines therefore two aims: the instrumental aim which now dominates much language teaching, i.e. using language for communication; and the humanistic aim which is often not adequately recognised, i.e. using language teaching to help our learners to understand others and themselves.

跨文化交际语言教学 (ICLT) 的基本概念

这一讲主要是关于跨文化交际语言教学中的基本概念的，并会区分传统语言教学和现代语言教学，然后讨论一下各种知识。首先我会谈语言教学，因为我想这是你们最熟悉的，然后再讲一下文化和语言文化的相关知识，最后给大家举一个例子。

两种知识

语言教学有传统和现代两种教学模式（Trim, 2012），无论是汉语、英语、法语还是其他语种教学都适用于这两种模式。在"传统"的教学模式下，学习语言是为了锻炼思维，过去在我们还没有很多国际交流的时候，中国人学习英语或者其他外语的目的是训练思维、锻炼大脑。但同时，学语言也是为

Fundamental Concepts in Intercultural Communicative Language Teaching (ICLT)

I want to begin this lecture on concepts with the distinction between traditional language teaching and modern language teaching, and then consider kinds of knowledge. In doing this I will begin by referring to the teaching of language because that's what you are, I assume, most familiar with. Then I'll talk about these kinds of knowledge for culture and languaculture. Finally I'll present an example.

Two Kinds of Knowledge

I start with the distinction of **two kinds of language teaching – traditional and modern** – (Trim, 2012) whichever language is being taught, Chinese teaching, English teaching, French teaching, and any foreign language teaching. 'Traditionally', the languages we learnt exercised the mind. When people learnt English or other languages in China in the past before we had lots of international communication, they learnt English to exercise the mind, and to make the mind think or work harder. Secondly, it was a matter of learning a foreign language in order to understand 'the culture'. 'The culture' in the past was above all equated with literature and philosophy. In China, people learnt English in order to read Shakespeare, or in other countries, people learnt Chinese in order to read Confucius. People learnt French to read Racine and Molière, and Descartes. The focus was therefore upon the written language; we learnt to read and write, and to translate, and I say 'we' because this was the way I learnt languages, and 'tradition' is still within living memory. And that was perfectly good as a purpose for language teaching before we had lots of international communication, lots of travel.

Now, travel and communication have become easy and relatively cheap, and today we have 'modern' language teaching where we have different purposes. We learn a foreign language to use it. It has instrumental purposes. We want to use

了进一步了解"文化",但是在过去"文化"与文学和哲学是画等号的。中国人学英语是为了读懂莎士比亚,而其他国家的人们学汉语是为了读懂孔子,学法语是为了读懂拉辛、莫里哀和笛卡尔。所以我们传统的关注点主要是书面语言,即能够读写和翻译,我说的是"我们",因为我也是这么学习语言的,而且对这种传统依然记忆犹新。在广泛的国际交流与旅行还未成形之前,这种教学目标不失为一种极好的选择。

但是现在,随着旅行与交流愈见实惠便捷,我们也随之转向了"现代"的教学模式。与传统模式的目的不同,我们学习一门外语是为了使用它。语言是工具。我们希望用语言进行交际。我们学一门外语是为了和来自不同文化的人进行交流,并不是为了读懂莎士比亚,因为莎士比亚已经故去了!所以"文化"这个词如今有了不同的含义。它不再是文学、哲学意义上的文化,而是日常生活、工作中所涉及的文化,这导致学一门外语主要是为了交谈。传统意义上的学外语主要是为了书写,现在则是口语更为重要。因此,即使写作仍具有工具性的作用,有时我们给予写作的关注度仍然不够。我们写电子邮件的语言就是口语和书面语的融合。即使现在人们也会写信或写报告,所以写作还是很重要的。

对口语的重视是传统语言学习和现代语言学习的一个重要差异,也是一个重要的出发点,但这并不是要丢弃传统,不是非此即彼,而是两者兼顾。学习语言既要考虑传统的目的,也要兼顾现代的目的。这是我们的出发点。

下面我想谈谈**不同的认知方式**(Ryle, 1945),这对于所有的教学都很重要,也包括语言教学。有两种知识:陈述性知识和程序性知识。换句话说,陈述性知识是"是什么的知识",就是我们通常认为的知识;而程序性知识是"怎么做的知识",或者说是"技能"。比如骑自行车。我会骑自行车。在我小的时候我通过反复尝试,骑上车,摔下来,学会了骑车。当时我不知道怎么骑,但是慢慢我学会了,而且永远不会忘记这种技能。我知道了"怎么做",我也知道了骑自行车的要点就是要一直在车上,上身挺直往前蹬,如果不蹬就要掉下来,但我不知道这是为什么。我学会了怎么骑自行车,但却不知道背后的科学原理,不知道能够解释为何不往前蹬就会摔下来的物理学原理。我掌握了骑自行车的技巧,却不知道关于骑自行车的知识,因为我不是物理学家。在学自行车中有两种类型的知识。

在语言教学上也是一样。我可以给大家举一些英语作为外语的教学案例,

it for communication. We learn a foreign language to talk to people from other cultures. In this perspective, we don't learn a foreign language to read Shakespeare, because he is dead! So the word 'culture' is different now. It means culture not in the sense of literature and philosophy, but culture in the sense of everyday life and everyday work, and this has led to the emphasis on learning a foreign language mainly for speaking. Traditionally, it was mainly for writing, and now it is mainly for speaking. As a consequence, sometimes we don't give enough emphasis to writing, even though writing is important even in instrumental terms. We use writing for e-mail, a kind of writing which is a mixture between spoken language and written language. Even today we still write letters, and we still write reports. And so writing is still important.

There is then a major difference between traditional language learning and modern language learning, which is important as a starting point, but it is not a matter of forgetting tradition. It is not a matter of either/or. It is a matter of both/ and, both learning languages for traditional purposes and for modern purposes. That is the starting point.

I want now to move to **different ways of 'knowing'** (Ryle, 1945). This is fundamental to all teaching and learning, also language teaching and learning. There are two kinds of knowing: declarative knowing and procedural knowing. In other words, 'knowing that', which is what we usually think of as knowledge; and 'knowing how', or in another word 'skill'. Take for example riding a bicycle. I know how to ride a bicycle. When I was little, I learnt how to ride a bicycle by experiment. I got on a bicycle, and I fell off, because I did not know how. But gradually I learnt how to ride a bicycle, and I have never forgotten. I 'know how', and I also 'know that' when riding a bicycle if you want to stay on, then you must stay upright, and move forward. If you don't move forward, then you fall off. But I don't know why. So I know how to ride a bicycle but I don't know the science, and the physics which would tell me why I would fall off if I don't move forward. I have skill in riding a bicycle, but I don't know

---

Traditional and modern

- Traditional = languages learnt for
  1) 'exercising the mind'
  2) accessing 'culture' = literature and philosophy
  → learn **written** language (to read and write – and translate)

- Modern = language learnt for
  – 'use' in communication
  – talking to people from other 'cultures' = everyday life/work
  → learn mainly **spoken** language – 'written' under-emphasised as reaction to past

NOT 'EITHER /OR' BUT 'BOTH/ AND'

也请大家想些汉语的例子，因为我只知道"你好"和"谢谢"这两个词，别的都不会。说到英语的例子，大家肯定都"知道"：在一般现在时中，第三人称单数的动词后要加 s，比如"I go"，但会说"he/she goes"，这是老师教给你们的语法。但是"知道怎么做"就大不相同了。我们不仅要知道语法规则，还要会用。然而很多人说英语时都知道这个语法规则，也就是说现在时第三人称的动词后要加 s，但是他们就是没有按规则出牌。所以我们要学会综合两种知识，即"是什么的知识"和"怎么做的知识"。然而"知道怎么做"并不简单，即使水平很高的英语学习者，有时在第三人称的动词之后还是不加 s。

我给大家再举一个例子：摩擦音。含有 th 的很多单词，如 the、that、this、those 里有摩擦音。我可以教给我的学生，th 是摩擦音，也就是说让他们"知道"th 是摩擦音。但是如何发出这个音就完全是另一回事儿了。每个人都能学会这是个摩擦音，但是他们仍然发不出它。我想在汉语教学中肯定也有类似的例子。在座诸位很多已经是老师了，你们在教学生的时候是不是要用汉语教语法规则，虽然反复地教，但学生还是经常会忘？就像在英语中教第三人称单数动词后要加 s 一样，虽然反复地教，然而到了实际运用中，大家还是不会用。

那么，"怎么做的知识"和"是什么的知识"有什么区别？首先，在知道怎么说和知道怎么写之间是有差异的。每个人都"知道"，第三人称单数后面的动词是要加 s 的，但在口语交际中经常不加 s，会说 he go，而不是说 he goes，但在书写时不会犯这样的语法错误，因为写的时候会有更多的时间在"知道是什么"和"知道怎么做"之间建立联系。作为老师，有时我们听到学生在口语中没有加 s，可能会感觉很失望。但即使是优秀的英语口语者也经常会犯这样的错误，所以我们对学生在说和写上的期待值应该不一样。学生在书写的时候，我们应该要求更高。我们期待学生的写作能力比口语强。

Relationship between 'that' and 'how'

- Are knowing '3rd person rule' and knowing how to say 'he goes' / writing 'she believes' related? How?
  - Is there a difference between 'knowing how to say' and 'knowing how to write'?
- How do we assess knowing that and knowing how (e.g. 3rd person rule or pronunciation of 'th')?

the knowledge about riding a bicycle, because I'm not a physicist. There are two kinds of knowledge in riding a bicycle.

This also applies to language teaching and learning. I can give you my examples from teaching English as a foreign language, and I have to ask you to think about Chinese, because I have two words in Chinese 你好 and 谢谢 . After that, I know nothing. So you have to think about examples in Chinese for yourself, but in English, as I am sure you remember, we 'know that' in the third person in the present tense, you put an 's' on the end of the verb: 'I go', but 'he/she goes'. That's a rule you learn from your teachers. But 'knowing how' is different; we have to know the rule but also use it. Yet many people who speak English 'know that' the third person verb finishes in an 's', but they don't do it. So we need to combine 'knowing that' and 'knowing how'. Yet 'knowing how' is not always easy. Even very advanced speakers of English often do not put 's' on the third person singular.

Let me take another example: the dental fricative. The pronunciation of 'the' 'that' 'this' 'those', and many words with 'th', involves a dental fricative. I can teach my learners that 'th' is a dental fricative, i.e. the knowing that 'th' is a dental fricative. Yet how to pronounce 'th' is a different matter. Everybody can learn the fact that this is a dental fricative, but they still don't produce it. I am sure there are similar examples in teaching Chinese. You teach students a rule in Chinese again and again, but they always 'forget'. The same for third person 's' in English, one can teach the 'knowing that' again and again with no apparent effect on 'knowing how'.

What then is the relation between 'knowing how' and 'knowing that'? First, there is a difference between knowing how to speak and knowing how to write. Learners know from an early stage in language learning that the third person ends in 's', but when they speak, even very good English speakers will often say 'he go'. However, when they write, they will not make that mistake. When we write, we have more time to make a link, a connection, between 'knowing that' and 'knowing how'. As teachers, we are perhaps disappointed when, in speaking, our learners do not produce the third person 's'. That is a disappointment, but it happens a lot even in excellent speakers of English and we should have different expectations of learners when they are speaking and when they are writing. When our learners write something, we should be more demanding. We should expect them to write better than they can speak.

Different expectations lead us to the question of **assessment**. How do we assess 'knowing that' and 'knowing how' and is it different? We can easily assess 'knowing that'. I can ask you 'How does the third person verb in English end?' If you tell me it ends in 's', you are correct and get full marks. If I ask you to talk to me, and you

不同的期待引出了**评估**的问题。如何来评估"知道是什么"和"知道怎么做"呢？有什么区别吗？我们可以很容易评估"知道是什么"，比如我可以问你们："第三人称单数的动词的词尾应该怎么变形？"如果你告诉我在词尾加 s，你就算学会了。但是，如果让你跟我交谈，你在口语中没有加 s，你说的是 he go，这是错的吗？是错的，但和确保我理解你的意思相比，这个语法错误就显得没那么重要了。虽然有语法错误，但是我能理解，所以我会说："好吧，在 10 分制下，我可以给你个 7、8 分。"但如果是在写作中，我希望你可以做得更好，因此我可能只会给你 5 分。我能理解你想表达的意思，但你犯了一个本该避免的语法错误。我们必须从不同的方面来考虑评估问题，关于这个话题我将在之后的讲座中详述。

能力

下面我将引入**能力**的概念以及能力与上述两种知识的关系。能力是"是什么的知识"与"怎么做的知识"这两者的结合。如果你知道第三人称单数的动词变形规则，你也可以这么去说，或者这么去写，那么你就具备了这种能力。

还有一个词叫"**交际性能力**"。交际性能力指的是能够把这两种知识结合在一起，**得体地**使用语言，也就是说**礼貌地**使用语言。比如你在英国的一家公司教汉语，你不仅需要让学生知道哪些语言形式是礼貌的，还需要教会他们得体或礼貌地使用语言。你要教一些在上司面前能够使用的礼貌用语，同时你也要教怎么去做，怎样是礼貌的，怎么样能够使用这些语言知识。

Competence

- Know that + know how = competence
- 'Communicative Competence' = using language appropriately ['politely']
- Knowledge that 'it is appropriate/polite to say/write ... when speaking in Chinese to your boss in Britain/USA/China/Japan/etc.
- Knowledge how to do it (and not feel awkward because of difference)
- 'Politeness' is surface of 'culture'

do not put an 's' on the end. If you say 'he go', then do I say that it's wrong? Yes it's wrong, but maybe it's not as important as making sure I understand what you mean. If you say to me 'he go London this morning', I understand. There's an error, but I understand. So maybe I say, 'Alright, you can have seven or eight marks out of ten.' But if you write to me 'he go London this morning', I will say that is not good, because in writing, I expect you to be better. In that case I will give you five out of ten. I understand, and that is important, but you've made a grammatical error in writing which you should have avoided. We have then to think about assessment in different ways, and I will talk more about assessment in a later lecture.

Competence

Now let's talk about the word **competence** and its relationship to 'knowing that' and 'knowing how'. Competence is 'knowing that' plus 'knowing how', the two together. If you know that the third person ends in 's' and you also say it, and write it, then you have competence.

Secondly, we have the phrase *communicative competence*, which refers to using the two kinds of knowledge and using language *appropriately*, or *politely*. Imagine you are teaching someone Chinese in a company in Britain, you teach them not just 'knowledge that' certain forms are polite, but you also teach them how to use the language politely or appropriately. You have to teach 'that' certain polite forms of speaking which are appropriate for the boss, and you also have to teach them how to do it, how to be polite, and how to use their 'knowledge that'.

Furthermore, they have to be able to do this without feeling strange, and feeling awkward. I return to my example at the beginning. When I say to my Chinese, Japanese, or South Korean students, they should call me 'Mike'; they often don't like to do so. They feel awkward. Using a foreign language politely and appropriately can sometimes feel awkward because it is different from politeness in our own language. That is because it is connected with our culture, with

　　此外，他们在做的过程中不应感到奇怪或尴尬。回到一开始的例子，我在教中国、日本或韩国的学生时，让他们叫我 Mike，他们不愿意，因为他们感觉很别扭。所以，礼貌和得体地使用外语，有时会让我们感觉有点尴尬，因为这不同于我们母语中的礼貌用语。这与文化相关，与通常的做法相关，即使是像称呼这样的小事。

　　我们现在从简单的知识和如何运用知识过渡到文化和情感层面，因为礼貌也是文化的一部分，但只是文化的表层，礼貌地使用语言只是文化的开端。但是，语言还不够，只教语言也是不够的。我给大家举个例子，我来自英国的大学，英国大学和中国大学一样，也要开很多会，会实在是太多了。开会时，我经常听到这么一句话，"我听到你说的了"，之后再接着说别的。人们常说"我听到你说的了"，但是，这句话里还有一些潜台词，而且大家也都明白，即"我虽然听见了，但不感兴趣"。因此说"我听见你说的了"，并不真正意味着我听进去了，而是说，我想尽量表现得礼貌一些，但是我对你讲的并不感兴趣。其他与会的英国教授可能就知道如果有一个人这么讲了，他的意思就是说他不感兴趣，因为这句话人们用得很多，所以大家可以相互理解，这是没有问题的。但是如果来了一个法国教授，他的理解可能就会有点不同。他可能会想："哦，他听见我说的了，这就意味着他在听我讲。"换句话说，这个法国教授完全误解了当时的状况。我想如果是一个中国教授的话，也会误解这句话。但我用这个法国教授的例子其实是想说明，实际上这并不是中国和西方的区别，即便是在西方国家内部，在欧洲内部，英国大学里的一个法国教授也会误解一些话的真正含义，也会存在文化的差异。

　　所以我们应该忘掉"西方"和中国的差异，因为并没有一个所谓的"东方"的概念。中日韩之间都存在着差别。当英国人、法国人、德国人，想到东方的时候，会觉得日本人和中国人是一样的。如果我觉得你是日本人的话，你可能会很不高兴，因为这就相当于我误解了你。如果你们认为我和所有的"西方人"一样，就是把我等同于美国人、德国人，如果这么讲的话大家也是在误解我。所以让我们忘记"西方"这个概念吧。我们要分别看不同的国家，即使在一个国家内部也存在着差别。

the way we normally do things, even little things like how to call somebody by their first name.

We are now beginning to move from simple 'knowledge', knowledge that and knowledge how, to matters of culture and feeling, because politeness is part of our culture. It is however only the surface of our culture. Language used politely is the beginning of culture, but language is not enough, and to teach only language is not enough. Let me give you an example. I am from a British university, and in a British university, as in Chinese universities I am sure, we have many meetings, too many meetings. In meetings I have often heard this phrase 'I hear what you say', and then blablabla. People say: 'I hear what you say.' Yet what they do not go on to say and what is nonetheless still present in the room is 'but I am not interested'. So the phrase 'I hear what you say' does not mean 'I hear what you say'. It means 'I am trying to be polite, but I am not interested in what you say'. A British person in the same meeting knows that the person who says 'I hear what you say' is not interested, because this is a phrase people use a lot and that is fine; we understand each other. However, if it were a French professor in the same meeting, he or she might understand differently. He/she might understand, 'Oh he says I hear what you say, that means he is listening to what I am saying'. In other words, the French professor misunderstands completely the situation. I think if it were a Chinese professor, it would be the same, but I take as an example a French professor, because it is not a matter of China and 'the West'. Even within 'the West', even within Europe, a French professor in a British university will misunderstand and have cultural differences.

So let us forget about 'the West' and China, because as you know, there is no such thing as 'the East'. There is a difference between China and Japan and South

Korea and so on. There is a similar problem in reverses that English people, French people, German people, think about 'the East' and think that Japanese are the same with Chinese. If I think that you are Japanese, you would not be very pleased, because you think I

BUT Language is not enough...

- Spoken text and unspoken text:
  - In a meeting in a British university: 'I hear what you say' [spoken] 'but I am not interested' [unspoken]
- Understood text:
- By a British professor = 'He is not interested'
- By a French professor = 'He is listening to what I am saying' [or a Chinese professor]

- NOT CHINA AND 'THE WEST' BUT WITHIN 'WESTERN COUNTRIES' [compare China and Japan, etc., not 'The East']

我们还要更进一步，因为语言本身还是不够的。礼貌是语言和文化之间的桥梁，尽管礼貌只是一个表层的东西。因此我们必须引入"**文化**"的概念，一个既熟悉又复杂的词。还有"**语言文化**"，这是个比较新的词，是近四五十年提出的新概念（Risager，2006）。

文化

"文化"是一个动词（Street，1993）。从语法上来讲，文化当然不是动词，它是一个名词。但是我要说"文化是一个动词"是个很好的表述，这是我的一个朋友在几年以前提出的。动词是关于做事情的，而文化也是关于做事情的，它是关于怎么做的知识。

文化是一个很难的词。有人说，它是英语里面最难的词之一，我想它在汉语、日语和其他语言里面，也是非常难的词。因此，我们看一下文化的部分含义，这部分含义对语言教师有重要意义。

作为语言教师，我们可以把文化看作事物。这种情况下文化是名词，相当于我们生产的产品。它是纪念碑，是书籍，是绘画，或者是社会产品，比如我们制定的社会法律也是社会产品，很难触及，不像我们去触摸一幅画、一本书那样简单，但仍旧是事物。教育体系、宗教也是事物，是社会的产物，也是人们**行为**的结果，所以文化就变成了动词，我们每天都在做的事情就是文化。我们每天生活在群体当中，隶属不同的群体。比如我属于我的家庭、职业群体、我所在的村庄，属于某一宗教团体，是国家公民，这只是几种不

would misunderstand you. If you think that I am the same as all 'Westerners', that I am the same as Americans, as Germans, then you would have understood me. So let us forget about 'the West'. We have to look at individual countries and even within each country there are differences.

I have said so far that language is not enough and politeness is the link between language and culture, although it is only the surface. This means that we need to consider the word 'culture', a familiar though complex word, and 'languaculture', a new word which has existed for only forty or fifty years (Risager, 2006).

Culture

'Culture' is a verb (Street, 1993). Grammatically, of course it is not a verb, it is a noun. But 'culture is a verb' is a good phrase, which one of my friends invented a few years ago. Verbs are about doing things, and culture is about doing things. It is about knowing how.

It is a difficult word. Somebody said it is one of the most difficult words in English and I guess it is a very complex word in Chinese, Japanese, and other languages as well. I propose therefore to look at part of the meaning of culture, the part which is important for language teachers.

As language teachers, we can think of culture as things. In that case, culture is a noun. It is what we produce. It is monuments. It is books, or paintings. Or it is social products; in society, we produce laws. Those are things. They are not so easily touched in the way we can touch a painting or a book, but they are still things. Education systems are things. Religions are things. They are social products, the outcome of what people *do* and that is why 'culture is a verb' is a good phrase because culture is something we do in everyday life, and in everyday life we live in groups. We all belong to different groups. We belong to 'my family', 'my profession', 'my village', 'my religion', and 'my country'; these are just a few groups. We belong to many groups, but let us talk about my profession and your profession as language teachers, or languaculture teachers. In that group, we do things because we do them as a member of the group. What do teachers do? They sit or stand in front of the class. That is something that teachers do; if you are a lawyer, you don't stand in front of a group of people in a classroom. You sit or stand in a court room. Lawyers do things, even little things, even simple things, differently to teachers. When teachers stand in front of students, they produce certain things together with learners. Lawyers produce different things. They produce discussion and eventually a verdict about someone in court. Whereas teachers and learners together produce

同类型的群体。我们属于很多群体，但是让我们谈一谈作为语言教师或语言文化教师的这个职业群体吧。在这样的群体里，我们是以群体中一员的身份来做事的。教师做什么？他们或坐或站在学生们面前，这是老师的做法。如果你是律师，就不会站在教室里，面对很多学生，而会坐或站在法庭里。律师与教师所做的事情大不相同，即便是最微小的事情也有天壤之别。教师站在学生面前，实际上就是和学习者一起创造一种教学结果，但是律师做的是另外一类事，他们进行辩论，然后得出最终的判决结果。而教师和学习者共同塑造了学习者群体。

任何群体都有其文化，我们以群体成员的身份做事。换句话说，文化是由行为组成的，由我们所做的事情组成，这是可以看到的表征。比如你来到法院，就可以看到谁是法官，谁是被告，谁是律师，以及他们各自的行为。尽管每个国家情况可能稍有不同，但总体上可以看出不同行为的差异。在大部分国家，如果大家走进教室，就可以看出来谁是老师，可以观察他们的行为举止。

但是在行为的背后，便是我们所珍视的价值观，就是我们认为重要的东西，还有指导我们去行动的信仰。比如作为教师，我们非常看重"学生应该学习"、"学习是一件好事"这样的观念，这对所有教师来说都是天经地义的。如果我们不重视这些观念，就不是教师了。即使站在教室前，如果不觉得学习是一件很好的事情，也不注重学习的意义，那么也不是老师。其次，作为教师，我们坚信人们会以某种方式学习。我们相信学习方法之一就是倾听，就像你们现在所做的这样。虽然不是唯一的一种，但这却是一种学习途径。这就是我们所坚持的信念：文化既涵盖了行为，也囊括了价值观和信念。

作为规则的文化——行为、价值观和信仰

我给大家举个例子。有一本关于英格兰人的书（Fox，2004），这里的英格兰人不是英国人，不是西方人，也不是苏格兰人、威尔士人、爱尔兰人，而只是生活在英格兰地区的人。书的作者观察英格兰人很长时间，观察他们如何行为处事。她是一位人类学家，观察之后就写了一本书，关于英格兰人的处事方式，换句话说就是关于英格兰的文化。她观察英格兰人的行为，发现他们的行为是有规则可循的。这本书非常复杂，我在这里就只给大家举一个最简短的例子。作者观察一些英格兰人在公交车站等车，他们常常彼此聊

learners who have learned something.

Every group has a culture, and we do things as members of a group. In other words, cultures are made up of behaviours, things we do, and that is what you can see. You can see – if you go into a law court – which is the judge, and which is the accused, and which is the lawyer, and what they are doing, and their behaviours. There may be differences from one country to another but you can see the differences in behaviours. In most countries, if you go into a classroom, you can see which person is the teacher, and you can see their behaviours.

However, behind what we do are ideas that we value, that we think are important, and the beliefs, which underlie what we do. For example, as teachers, we value the idea that learners should learn, and that learning is a good thing; that is something which is fundamental to all teachers. If someone doesn't value that, then they are not teachers. Even if they stand in front of the class, if they don't think that learning is good, they do not value learning, then they are not teachers. Secondly, as teachers, we believe that people learn in certain ways. We believe that one way of learning is to listen, as you are doing now. Not the only way, but it is one way. That is a belief that we have. Culture is therefore a matter of behaviour and value and belief.

Culture is a verb...

- 'One of the two or three most difficult words in English' [and Chinese?]

- Culture as things – material products [monuments, books, paintings, etc.] OR social products [e.g. laws, education systems, religions, etc.]... – the 'product' of what people do...
- Culture as everyday life – what a group of people (my family, my profession, my age group, my village, my region, my country– ANY GROUP I BELONG TO) do...
- Culture = behaviours AND values and beliefs which determine [rule] behaviours

Culture as rules – behaviours, values and beliefs

Let me give you an example. From a book about the English (Fox, 2004). The English, not the British, not the westerners, not the Scottish, not the Welsh, not the Irish, but only the English. The author of the book observed English people for a long time, many years. She observed what they do. She is an anthropologist. She then wrote a book about what English people do. In other words, about English culture. She observed their behaviour and that in their behaviour there are certain rules. The book is very complicated, and I have taken a very simple example, the simplest and shortest example. The author observes English people at a bus stop waiting for a bus, and when people are waiting at a bus stop, they often talk to each

天，不是总聊天，是常常聊天，典型话题就是天气。他们会说，"今天真是够冷啊？"，然后对方会回答，"对啊，谁说不是呢？"。大多数情况下人们都会这样交换信息。但是如果大家更为仔细地分析一下就会发现，这些都不是真正意义上的问句，只是用了问句的形式，并不是真正的疑问，只是一种问候的方式。当他们说，"今天真是够冷啊？"，他们并不是说真的冷，而是在说，"我想跟你聊两句，你愿不愿意和我聊天？"如果你回答说，"对啊，谁说不是呢？"，其实就是在说，"好啊，我们边等车边聊天吧。"这就意味着行为背后是有一些规则的。首先规则之一就是"相互性规则"。你必须要做出反应，如果你不反应就是没有礼貌。而如果你没有礼貌，就不属于这种文化，所以一定要做出反应，但是这不只是反应的问题，反应过程中还要有认同，这才是正常的反应。如果你说，"不对，我觉得今天挺暖和的"，这就是反常的反应了。人们会觉得很奇怪，很好笑。如果我这样说了，我是不礼貌的，但是我完全可以这么回答。我的回答依然表示"好的，我们聊天吧"，但在这里情况就复杂得多了。所以第二个规则是"语境规则"。在这个语境下，你可以把谈论天气作为一种问候，也可以通过谈论天气来打破僵局，然后再谈其他内容。你可以谈公共汽车，可以说，"这个车老是慢，39路公共汽车总是晚点，是不是？"。我们可以谈论，那很好，是我们珍惜的。如果39路车还没有来，你还是想继续这场对话，但是你又不知道说什么，那就可以接着谈天气。所以天气就是一个"默认"的话题，总是可以回到天气的话题。

大家可以观察中国的公交车站，人们都用什么样的方式搭讪。也许你可以总结出中国或者是北京的规则，也许北京不同于上海、广东或是其他地方，但是你可以推导出一套行为规则来。

为什么是这样？我们的行为背后有着某些信念，即我们相信其他英格兰人，或者其他人，像我们一样喜欢彼此交谈。同时，我们珍视在一起的感觉，希望能通过交谈创造一种社会温情，这是英格兰潜在的信念和价值观。可能在中国也是一样，有些行为、价值观和信仰可以跨越国界，大家应该比我更了解。

但是我想说的是关于刚才英格兰的规则，即社会群体行为的规则。无论家庭、职业还是其他层面，总会有规则存在。然而这些规则其实是一些约定俗成的传统，而不是法律，不像语法一样，不像英语中第三人称单数动词的

other. They do not always talk but often; this is important as we shall see. They will talk about the weather. They might say 'Isn't it cold?' and the answer is 'Yeah. Isn't it?' That's the typical exchange most of the time people will say. However, if we look at the exchange more carefully, these are not questions. They look like questions, but they are in fact greetings; they are behaviours of greeting. They say 'It's cold, isn't it?' but they are saying 'I'd like to talk to you. Will you talk to me?'. If you say 'Um yes, isn't it?', then you are saying 'Yes. Let's have a little chat while we are waiting for the bus.' This means that there are certain rules behind this behaviour. First of all, there is what the author calls the 'reciprocity rule'. You have to respond. If you don't respond, you are not polite. And if you are not polite, you are not part of this culture. But it is not just a matter of responding. You have to respond by agreeing. That is the normal response. If you say 'Um I think it is warm', there is something odd and people often laugh as you are doing in my audience now, because it is an abnormal, unusual response. If I say this, I am not being polite, but I can respond like this. If I do, I am still saying 'Yes, let's talk', but it will be a more complex situation. So there is also a second rule, a 'context rule'. In this context, you can use a question about the weather as a greeting. You can use it therefore as an 'ice-breaker'. Let us 'break the ice' and then we can talk about other things. We can talk about the bus. We can talk about things like 'These buses are always late, aren't they?' or 'The No. 39 is always late, isn't it?'. We can talk and that is 'good', something we value. However, if No. 39 does not come and still does not come, and we want to keep talking, but we don't know what to say, then we start talking about the weather again. So the topic is a 'default' topic; you can always go back to the weather.

Now you can observe people in China at bus stops and see what the rules are. You may be able to work out the rules in China or in Beijing, because maybe Beijing is different from Shanghai, Guangdong, or somewhere else, but you can probably work out the rules of behaviour.

Why do we do follow rules in this way? We have certain beliefs behind our behaviour; we believe that other English people, and

Watching the English – K. Fox 2004

- BEHAVIOUR
- Rules of English weather speak:
- English person at a bus stop speaking to another [English or Chinese or... =]
  - 'Oh, isn't it cold?' 'Um, yes, isn't it?'

NOT QUESTIONS BUT GREETINGS [SPEECH ACTS/BEHAVIOURS]
  - 'I'd like to talk to you – will you talk to me?'
  RULES OF BEHAVIOUR:
    - Reciprocity rule – respond!
    - Agreement rule – agree or risk complexity
    - Context rule – use as greeting, as ice-breaker for further talk, as 'default' to fill gap
- BELIEF
  - We English believe that other human beings are like us
- VALUE
  - English people value creating social warmth [by talking to others]

后面总是要加 s 一样。我们说的这种社会交际的规则，是远超于此的。关于文化的这些规则是约定俗成的，就是说**大多数人在大多数时间都会这么做，但是不总是这样**，所以我们要避免模式化，不应该说所有的英格兰人都愿意在公交车站谈天气，这是不对的。我们必须要非常谨慎，不要理所当然地认为规则一成不变，永远被遵循。并不是所有的中国人在所有的时刻都遵守同一个规则。而是在某些情况下，**大多数人在大多数时间都遵循这些规则**。这些规则可以通过"是什么的知识"来传授，但是我们要注意学生在了解相关知识时，应该知道这个规则是在大多数时间适用于大多数人的，而不是每时每刻都在起作用。

> 'Rules' about what to do in a social group (e.g. my family; my profession; my ethnic group... my nation, etc.)
>
> - BUT RULES ARE CONVENTIONS NOT LAWS
>   - Not like grammar rules!!
>   - SOME ENGLISH PEOPLE FOLLOW THESE RULES...
>   - AVOID STEREOTYPES (OF 'THEM' AND 'US' – not all Chinese do the same thing all the time!!)
>
> - WE LEARN ABOUT WHAT **SOME** PEOPLE DO
>   - Some = 'most of the people most of the time'

所以规则有三种，有一些是我们有意识地说出来的规则。如果你为人父母，就会教孩子一些规则，比如英国父母会告诉孩子用手指人是不礼貌的。孩子小的时候经常用手指人，但这是不礼貌的，所以我们会告诉他们这个规则：不要用手指人。这是一个有意识的规则，所有的英国人都是这样做的，不知道在中国是否也是如此。

有一些规则是半意识的，没有说出来的。如果有人打破这个规则，我们就会觉得有一些不舒服或尴尬，我们注意到可能有些事情不太对，这才意识到这个潜在的规则。比如在公交车站上我说，"太冷了，是不是？"旁边有人说，"不，我觉得很热"，我们当时就会觉得很尴尬。然后我们大笑或用其他方式表示尴尬。如果意识到其他人没有遵循这个规则，这个规则就是半意识的。还有一种情况，我们到其他的国家或同一国家中的不同文化区域，或

perhaps other human beings, are like us. They like to talk. And we value this idea of being together, of creating social warmth by talking to each other. These are the underlying beliefs and values in England. Perhaps this is also the case in China and some of behaviours, values and beliefs may be international; you know this better than I.

The author was however giving the rules of the English, the rules about what to do in a social group. Whether it's your family, your profession or whatever, there are rules. Rules are however conventions; they are not laws. They are not like grammar rules. In English, the 's' is always expected at the end of the third person verb. If you say 'he go', it's wrong; the rule is like a law. Rules about culture are not laws but conventions, i.e. *what most people do most of the time, but not always*. We have to avoid stereotypes, to avoid thinking that all English people at the bus stop talk about the weather. That is not true. We have to be careful not to think that these rules are followed by everyone all the time and everywhere. Not all Chinese people follow the same rules all the time, but in some circumstances, *most people most of the time* follow the rules. Such rules can be taught and learnt as 'knowledge that', but we have to be careful that when our learners acquire such 'knowledge that', they know that most people most of the time do certain things, but not all the time.

Rules/conventions are of three kinds. There are those which are conscious and spoken. If you are a parent, then you teach your children certain rules. English parents tell children that it's not polite to point at people. Children often do so

是进入不同的行业，比如我们作为老师去和律师进行交谈，我们会感到有一些不适应，因为有些规则是半意识的，我们只是一知半解，只有在事情出现差异时才会察觉。

还有一些规则是完全潜意识的，经常与我们的情感相连，但对我们而言非常重要。当我们经历"文化冲击"时，会感到很奇怪。不管是在同一个国家，还是在不同的国家、不同的行业，一个完全不同的文化语境会让我们感到难受。这是因为总有一些潜意识的规则，我们不断学习却不断忘记。

Rules

- Some rules are CONSCIOUS and SPOKEN — parents teach their children how to behave
- Some rules are SEMI-CONSCIOUS and UNSPOKEN — we notice them when they are NOT followed OR when we are in a different culture
- Some rules are UNCONSCIOUS — but affect us deeply/emotionally

---

这三种规则适用于所有的社会群体。在你的家庭里，你学会了怎样的礼貌规则呢？你是不是知道了用手指人是不礼貌的？你是否认为善意的谎言也是谎言？也就是说你知道有些谎言可能会帮助人们感觉好一些。可能有的人会说，"我头都秃了"，你会说，"不，我觉得你的头发很漂亮"，虽然并不是很漂亮，但是你也会用善意的谎言使别人舒服。在某些国家、某些家庭，这种善意的谎言是礼貌的表示，但是在另外一些家庭或国家，善意的谎言是不礼貌的。你应该开诚布公，非常诚实，这对那些惯常于使用善意谎言的人来说是很不自在的。我们在家庭环境下学到了一些规则，知道哪些规则在家庭中是最为重要的。比如在你家里谁是最终说话定夺的人，是父亲吗？最后是他拍板，还是孩子说了算？不同的家庭有不同的情况，不同的国家也存在差异。

简言之，每一个社会群体都有其自身文化。在我们进入某个社会群体之前，我们学会了这些规则，这些规则告诉我们如何去做。比如你想教书，你就要融入教师群体并接受培训。你要学习这个群体中的行为准则、信念和价值观。

when they are little, but it is impolite. So we tell them the rule: do not point at people. That's a conscious rule that we know. All of us do the same in England. I don't know if it would be the same in China.

Other rules are semi-conscious and unspoken, and we only notice them when somebody breaks the rule, when we feel a little awkward, a little uncomfortable, and we know that something is slightly wrong. At the bus stop, if I say, 'It's cold, isn't it?', and the other person says, 'No, I think it's warm', then we feel awkward, and we laugh or show some other signs of feeling awkward. We realise that there are rules which the other person is not following, semi-conscious rules. Therefore, when we go to a different country or a different culture even within the same country, a different region of the same country, or a different profession, and we teachers begin to talk with lawyers, then we feel a little uncomfortable, because we notice that there are things that are semi-conscious, which we half know, and which we notice when things are different.

Thirdly, there are rules which are unconscious, but which are very important to us, often linked to our emotions. That's when we feel strange, when we have what is sometimes called 'culture shock'. We sometimes feel ill in a different cultural setting, in the same country or in a different country, in a different profession, because there are deep rules which you learn but then forget.

These three kinds of rules apply in all social groups. In your family, what rules did you learn about being polite? Did you learn it's impolite to point? Did you learn that telling a white lie is wrong? In other words, telling a lie but it's a lie to help people feel comfortable. Somebody says, 'Oh my hair is all wrong'. You say, 'No, no, you look wonderful.' Even though it is not true, that's a white lie, and in some countries, in some families, white lies may be polite, whereas in other families or other countries, white lies are impolite. In that case people are more 'open' or 'honest', and that causes a strange feeling for those who would normally tell a white lie. We learn these rules in the family. We learn beliefs about what is important in our family. For example, who should have the last word in your family? Should it be the father of the

---

Culture and social groups

- in your family
  - what RULES have you learnt/taught about 'being polite' or about 'telling white lies' and what values lie beneath them

  - what BELIEFS have you learnt/taught about family hierarchies e.g. who should have 'the last word' – and what values lie beneath
  - DISCUSS

  - Every social group has its culture... we learn **rules of what to do** as we enter it (e.g. 'enter' family, begin school, join profession, leisure group)

有些规则是有意识的，有些是半意识的，还有些是无意识的，你学习之后就"忘"了。你在接受教师培训的时候会学到一些规则，或者在参加过的某个兴趣小组中学到一些规则。想想你喜欢的一项体育运动吧。假如你喜欢徒步登山，你便会知道和其他驴友见面的时候该怎么打招呼，怎样做才是礼貌的。

国家文化

不同的群体有不同的行为方式、不同的价值观和不同的信念。语言教师总是对民族群体这个概念很感兴趣，即将某种语言作为母语的人群。那是不是有一种所谓民族文化的概念呢？有没有"中国文化"这个概念呢？我们在教汉语的时候是不是也在教中国文化呢？在语言教学中，我们通常假定是有一种国家文化的，因为我知道大家在学习英语的时候，可能学到了"美国人这么做，美国人那么想，英国人这么想"。我们是不是能够这么说呢？是否意味着存在民族文化呢？

为了回答这个问题，我们有必要从一个新的角度考虑一下"社会群体"或是"社区"这个概念了。实际上存在两种群体或社区。一种是我们通过亲身经历了解到的。比如我们生活在家庭中，知道家庭成员的情况。同理，我们也知道体育俱乐部的那些人，知道学校里所有人的情况。这些是你"亲身经历的群体"。还有一个群体是我们"想象的群体"。比如，我们不认识所有的汉语教师，但他们仍然构成了一个群体，而且因为我们知道它属于一个社会群体，所以我们知道每一位汉语教师群体里的教师，都会按照其共有的规则和信念行事，但是我们不认识所有的教师，因此这种群体被称为"想象的群体"（Anderson，1991）。这一表达适用于汉语教师这一职业。我们因认同于这个想象的群体而获得了一种想象的区域性身份，也许在中国，用"省"这个字比用"区域"更为妥当。

同样的道理也适用于国家。你不可能认识所有的中国人，但是你可以假想你是一个大群体的一分子，这个群体就是中国人的群体。你可以假想自己与这个群体有一些共通的价值观，比如教育理念。即使在中国这么大的国家，学校与学校之间也有其共通之处：有同样的课程设置。教育制度使我们成为中国人或是英国人，我们共享这些经验，以及对于这些假想社区的认知。大众传媒也反复强调我们的归属。我们都会看国家电视台的节目，关心国家大

family who has 'the last word', who decides? Should it be the child or the children? It varies from family to family. And it varies from country to country.

In short, every social group has its culture. The rules tell us what to do, and we learn them as we enter the social group. If you think about teaching, you entered a group of teachers when you were trained; you learnt the rules of behaviour and the beliefs and values behind them. Some of them are conscious, some of them semi-conscious, and some of them unconscious, rules you observed and learnt and then 'forgot'. You learned the rules as you were trained as a teacher. Or imagine a leisure group. Think of whatever sport you like. For example you like to go walking in the hills with a 'walking group' and you learn what is polite to do when you meet other walkers.

National culture

I have argued then that all kinds of groups have rules about behaviour, and values and beliefs which lie beneath them. Language teachers have always been interested in national groups, i.e. the large groups of people who are native speakers of the language in question. Is there then a national culture? Is there a Chinese culture? Can we teach Chinese culture when we teach Chinese language? In language teaching, we often assume that there is and I am sure that when you learnt English you learnt that 'The Americans do this. The Americans think that. The British think this'. Can we really say such things and imply that there are national cultures?

In order to answer this question, we need to think about social groups – or social communities, to use a different phrase – again, in a new way. There are two kinds of group or community. There are groups or communities, which we can experience and know personally. For example, we experience life in our family. We know all the people in our family through direct experience. Similarly, we know all the people in our sports club, handball, football, directly. We know all the people in our school directly. Those are examples of an 'experienced community'. The second kind of community is an 'imagined community'. For example, we do not know all the teachers of Chinese by direct experience, but it is still a community or group, and because it is a social group, we know that everybody behaves according to the shared rules and has the same beliefs. So they belong to what is called an 'imagined community' (Anderson, 1991) and that expression applies to professions like teachers of Chinese, it applies to regional groups to which we belong. We have a regional identity by identifying with the imagined regional community – in China maybe I should use the word 'province' instead of 'region'.

It also applies to the nation. You cannot know all the Chinese, but you can

事，接受国家的理念和政策，并且知道成千上万的人做着和我们一样的事情。所以国家群体是存在的，只不过是一个带有文化色彩的想象的共同体，尽管其文化是由主流群体来设定的。主流群体决定了学校的课程设置、媒体的所有权等等。这些都是由"主流群体"决定的，我们知道在英国，这个群体就是中产阶级，我在这里就不对中产阶级进行定义了。但是英国的中产阶级会决定课程设置，从而塑造国家文化。工人阶级虽然没有同样的文化认同，但是他们必须去学校学习，到了学校也就学习了这种文化，也就成了这个群体的一部分。多数情况是这样的。但是有些人不会接受所有的文化，有些人或多或少会抵制这种主流文化。不过这种想象中的主流文化正是我们努力去教授的文化。

A national culture?

- 2 kinds of social groups/communities
  - Experienced community – family, port club, school
  - Imagined community – profession, region, nation
    - Created by education system, mass media...
- National culture defined by 'dominant group', i.e. who decides curriculum, who owns media, etc. and accepted by **most (but not all) for most (but not all) of the time**

语言与文化

语言和文化是不可分割的——这就是我们最后要提到的基本概念。中国人打招呼经常说，"吃了吗？"，英语直译是"Have you eaten?"，但它只是文化表层的礼貌表述。还有一些语言表达反映出深层次的文化含义，比如"**道**"这个字是很难翻译成英语的。"表层词汇"和"深层词汇"都是语言和文化的组成部分，所以现在我们可以来谈"语言文化"，这个词可能很难翻译，但我们作为语言教师可以通过这个词表示我们不光是语言教师，还是文化教师。我们要把教授"是什么的知识"和"怎么做的知识"的教学法运用到语言文化的能力教学中去。

imagine that you are a member of a very large group of people called 'the Chinese' and you can imagine that you share something. That 'something' is created by going to school, for even in China which is the largest nation, nonetheless schools have something in common: they all have the same curriculum. We learn about our country and nation and the education system makes us into Chinese or, in my case, English. We identify with and share an imagined community. The mass media also tell us what we belong to. We all watch national television, national news and so on, and accept the national view, knowing that we are sharing it with millions of others. So a national community does exist but it's an imagined community with its culture, although closer analysis shows that national cultures are often dominated by one group of people within the imagined community. The dominant group decide, for example, what's in the school curriculum, they own and decide what is to be in the media. All of those things are decided by the 'dominant group'. In Britain, I would say it is the English middle class group of people which I won't try to define now. They decide what goes into the curriculum and into the national culture. Some people from the working class group may not share that culture, but they have to learn it when they go to school, so they become part of the dominant culture. 'Most of the people, most of the time'. But some people do not accept all of it. And some people are, in a small or large way, rebels against the dominant culture. But nonetheless there is an imagined national culture which we might therefore try to teach.

Language and culture

Language and culture are inseparable – this is the final fundamental concept. The way you greet people – 'Have you eaten?' is the English translation of Chinese way of greeting – is surface culture politeness, and is the way that we talk to each other. Other aspects of language reflect deep culture. The word *Dao* for example is difficult to translate into English. There are 'surface' words and 'deep' words, which are part of our language and culture, and to reflect this we can talk about 'languaculture',

---

LANGUACULTURE

- Language and culture are inseparable
  - We learn what to do by talking [conscious and unconscious]
  - Culture is language → 'languaculture'

- 'Greeting' [have you eaten] = 'everyday'(surface) culture = behaviour / beliefs / values

- 'Dao' = 'deep' culture = beliefs / values / behaviours

在传统的语言教学里，我们教授"是什么的知识"。汉语老师会说，"中国人这么做"，"中国人那么说"，他们讲授中国人的信仰，比如"道"。这是一种传统的语言教学方法，教语法的时候也是这样，讲的是"是什么的知识"。那么讲授"怎么做的知识"的现代教学又该如何做呢？教授"怎么做"在语言文化中有怎样的意义？这意味着我们要教学生去遵循中国人的习惯或传统，比如以中国人的方式来打招呼。

大家也许会教学生理解"道"这个字。它的意思是什么？"道"对于中国人和中国文化而言是一个非常深奥的概念，只教给学生怎么打招呼还远远不够，你还得教他们用"道"的方式去思考。

我们在教给学生得体的语言以及如何使用语言的过程中，也许能教学生了解适当的语言文化。我们还需要教他们如何去用中国人的方式进行思考。

但这其实是有问题的。如果你只教语言，语言本身是中性的，不附加任何的信仰和价值观，但是文化却代表着行为、价值观和信仰。所以如果你教学生说"吃了吗"这样一种中国人打招呼的方式，这是表层的，是礼貌用语，是所有人都可以接受的。但如果你教学生用中国人的方式去思考，去接受中国人的信仰和价值观，这就复杂得多。因为语言文化并不是中立的。如果大家把中国的价值观教给越南人、美国人或英国人，这是不是就意味着要他们抵制自己的价值观呢？这是一个重要的问题，但我并不知道答案。我是教师，但我仍然不知道问题的答案，这是留给大家思考的问题。

Compare language competence with languaculture competence

- Language competence is neutral
  – no beliefs/values

- BUT CULTURE IS BELIEFS/VALUES/BEHAVIOURS
  – LEARNING HOW TO FOLLOW CHINESE CONVENTIONS
  = ACCEPTING CHINESE VALUES

- Languaculture competence is not neutral
  – Accept Chinese values = Reject (Vietnamese, American, etc.) values (?)

a word which may be
difficult to translate, but
a word which we can use
as language teachers to
say that we are teachers
not only of language but
of languaculture. We are
languaculture teachers,
and we can apply our
pedagogical 'knowing
that' and 'knowing how'
to teach competence in a languaculture.

Traditionally, in traditional language teaching, we taught 'knowledge that'. Chinese teachers taught statements like 'the Chinese do this', 'the Chinese say that', and they taught knowledge about Chinese beliefs, and words like *Dao*. We used to teach in the same way that we taught grammar as 'knowledge that'. But what about 'modern' teaching, where we are also teaching 'knowing how' in language? What would teaching 'knowing how' in languaculture mean? It would mean that we teach people to follow the Chinese rules or conventions. So that for example you teach your learners to greet in the Chinese way.

Maybe you also teach your learners to understand the word *Dao*, and what it means, and that it is something which is very deep among Chinese people and in Chinese culture. You may then try to teach them not just 'knowing how' to greet but also 'knowing how' to think in a *Dao* way.

Just as we teach students appropriate language and how to use it, we may teach appropriate languaculture, and maybe we also teach them how to think in a Chinese way.

But there are problems. If you teach language, that's neutral. Language has no values or beliefs attached to it. But culture is beliefs, values and behaviours. So if you teach your learners to greet 'have you eaten' in Chinese, that's surface. That's politeness. And that's acceptable to everybody. But if you teach your students to think in a Chinese way, to have Chinese beliefs, to accept Chinese values, then that's a much more problematic question. Because languaculture is not neutral. If you teach Vietnamese learners, American learners or British learners Chinese values, does that mean that they reject their own values? That's an important question and I don't know the answer. I may be the teacher but I don't know the answer. So that's for you to think about.

总结

总结一下，我列出了一些关键词："使陌生变熟悉，使熟悉变陌生"，或者说，"以他者的眼光来看待我们自己""以全新的视角看待自我、看待他人"。这些就是人文教育的关键，是我们在语言教学中可以完成的目标，也是大学英语课程的目标之一。

举例来说，不同国家的世界地图并不相同。在中国版的世界地图里，中国位于世界的中心；在法国版的地图里，中国就位于右手边了，成了世界的边缘，但实际上世界是没有中心的；在澳大利亚版的地图里，澳大利亚就在中心靠上的位置，但其实没有上下之分。所以你可以从不同的视角来看这个世界。

Keywords

- To make the strange familiar and the familiar strange
- To see ourselves as others see us
- To decentre – to see the reality from a new perspective

- EXAMPLE

每个人都以自己为中心，从自己的角度出发看世界，而这种思维模式不仅仅在看地图时才会出现，在历史的发展进程中也是如此。

因此教师就面临一种困境。如果一位汉语教师教越南学生，他是不是该让学生站在中国人的立场上来审视他们自身？是不是让他们像中国人那样了解中国呢？换句话说，学会如何打招呼只是表层的文化，而学会运用中国人的价值观去思考和行动，这就是深层的文化了。是不是一定要在文化与文化之间一分高下呢？中国文化就是要优于越南文化？还是说越南文化要超越中国文化？这些都是我们需要思考的问题。

举例

最后，我给大家举一个具体的例子，帮助你们理解我刚才所讲的概念。

Summing Up

To sum up what I have said, here are some key words and phrases: 'To make the strange familiar, and the familiar strange' or 'to see ourselves as others see us' or 'to see ourselves and other people from a different perspective'. These are the keys to the humanistic education which we can achieve in language teaching and which is presented as one of the aims of College English.

For example, the world map is seen in different ways in different countries. In a Chinese map of the world, China is in the middle, while in a French map of the world, China is on the right side, on the edge of the world. As a matter of fact, the world has no middle. Also, in an Australian map of the world, Australia is in the middle and at the top. And yet there is no top. So you can see the world from different points of view.

Everyone sees the world from their own perspective with themselves 'in the middle', and not just as symbolised in maps of the world – the same process takes place in history for example.

So the teacher has a dilemma. Should you as Chinese teachers teach for example your Vietnamese learners to see themselves as Chinese people see them? To know China like the Chinese? In other words, to know how to greet – that's surface culture. To know how to think and act in a Chinese way

> ### The teacher's dilemma/question/puzzle...
>
> • Should (Chinese) teachers teach (Vietnamese/American, etc.) learners
>   ○ To see themselves as Chinese see them...
>
>   ○ To know China like the Chinese =
>   ○ (a) to know that/about (e.g. greeting and *dao*)
>   ○ (b) to know how (e.g. to greet) - surface
>   ○ (c) to know how (e.g. to act with *dao*) - deep
>   ○ (d) to see 'ours' or 'theirs' as better
>
> • Discuss...

with Chinese values – that's deep culture. To see ours or theirs as better, ours the Chinese better than yours the Vietnamese? Yours the Vietnamese better than ours the Chinese? These are all questions for you to think about.

An Example

Finally, I am going to give you an example to make concrete everything I have said so far. This is an example of teaching English in Bulgaria, in Eastern Europe in 1998. It's quite some time ago now, but it could be yesterday, although you will see

这是 1998 年在东欧国家保加利亚进行英语教学的例子。这个教学实例虽然已经有些年头了，但即使是昨天也完全可能发生同样的事情，过一会儿你们就会明白为什么。1998 年是一个关键的时间点。一位教师设计了教学目标，我之后会专门再讲教学目标。当时正值 12 月，圣诞节将近，所以她想教给学生保加利亚的圣诞节传统。她的目标是让学生了解1990年以后的保加利亚，她将比较一下英国和保加利亚的圣诞节传统以及相关的文化传统，这就意味着她一方面要教"是什么的知识"，一方面还要教"怎么做的知识"。最后她要让学生们通过开展"调研"形成自身对圣诞节的认识。

BRITISH AND BULGARIAN CHRISTMAS CARDS: A RESEARCH
PROJECT FOR STUDENTS
Krassimira Topuzova (Bulgaria) - 1998

Objectives were:

- show whether Bulgarian Christmas tradition has changed – after 1990 (= 'knowing that')
- compare with British tradition and introduce other cultural issues (= 'knowing how')
- 'research': analysing data, form concepts, draw conclusions (= 'knowing how')

所以，课程开始之前她就跟学生说："下周我们就要过圣诞节了，我想让大家都去商店买一两张圣诞贺卡，然后我想请大家观察一下店里面的其他人。"这位老师让学生观察商店里其他保加利亚人的行为，看他们在做什么，遵守什么样的规则，多大年龄，男性还是女性，买了什么等等。

第三步是在回学校后的第一节课上进行的。学生观察之后回到学校，这个老师说："请在小组内讨论，我希望你们相互展示一下自己买到的圣诞贺卡，聊一聊贺卡本身，同时练一下英语，然后提问。每个人必须提问，比如谁买了圣诞卡，多大规格等等。"这些都是简单的语言问题：圣诞贺卡有多大？上面有什么图案？谁印制的？等等。

然后这个老师说："我想让大家谈一谈为什么你们会买圣诞贺卡？为什么其他人会买圣诞贺卡？圣诞贺卡对保加利亚人的意义是什么？你们会把圣诞贺卡寄给谁？你会在上面写什么？"

why it is important to know that it was in 1998. The teacher planned her teaching by objectives, which are words I will come back to later. She wanted to teach her learners about Bulgarian Christmas. She was teaching English in December as Christmas approaches. Her objectives were to teach her learners about Bulgaria after 1990. She was going to compare British traditions of Christmas and other cultural issues which means that she was going to teach some 'knowledge that' and some 'knowledge how'. Finally she was also going to teach them how to find out for themselves about Christmas, to carry out 'research'.

Let's move to the details. Before the lesson started, she said to the students, 'Okay, next week we are going to do Christmas. I want you all to go to the local shop and buy one or two Christmas cards. And then I want you to observe other people in

Organisations of the project

* *Before lessons start*
  – each student to go to a shop and buy one Christmas card they'd like to post for Christmas.
* – in shop, observe: who buys cards - age, sex, nationality - how many do they buy - which cards sell more and which less?
* – school, exhibited cards and explained why he/she had bought a particular card: price, size or colour OR images and messages.

the shop.' She asked her learners to observe other Bulgarian people in a shop, and what they were doing, what rules they seemed to be following, how old they were, male or female, what they bought and so on.

The third step was the first lesson at school, when she asked them 'Talk in your small groups. I want you to show Christmas cards that you've bought, and I want you to talk about them, to talk to each other, and to practice your English. So you have to ask questions. Who buys Christmas cards? And you have to talk about the size of the Christmas cards. Using these questions.' These are all simple language questions. What sizes are your Christmas cards? What pictures are there? Who printed them? And so on.

She continued, 'And then I want you to talk

In the classroom: – groups of 5/6 in order to analyse the cards.

* WHO BUYS CHRISTMAS CARDS?
  – 1.What age, sex, occupation are they?
  – 2.Are they local people or tourists?
  – 3.How many cards do they buy?
* WHAT CHRISTMAS CARDS?
  – 1.What size and format are they?
  – 2.What images are included?
  – 3.Who printed them?
  etc.
* WHY BUY CHRISTMAS CARDS?
  – 1.What do Christmas cards mean to Bulgarians?
  – 2.Why do they buy them?
  – 3.Who do they send them to?
  – 4.What do they write on them?

这些问题能帮助学生去思考他们在购买圣诞贺卡时所遵循的规则。这些规则可能不是有意识的，而是半意识的。他们不得不思考一下，"为什么我每年都要这么做？我要把贺卡寄给谁或者不寄给谁？这些都是我经常遵循的规则"。老师让学生用英语聊这些问题，他们作为保加利亚人是怎么回应这些问题的。你也可以请自己的外国学生用汉语来讲讲他们作为美国人或者其他国家的人都做一些什么样的事情。

老师随后说："好，现在我们把贺卡分类。我希望你们想一想都买了哪类贺卡，可以按照贺卡上的图片或是根据上面写的文字进行分类，然后看看你们各自手里都有什么样的贺卡。"

- **Second stage: classification cards into types**, according to the images and messages -

  following types emerged:

  — <u>Traditional Bulgarian Christmas cards</u> - illustrating the traditional Christmas table

  — <u>Religious Christmas cards with Biblical images</u> - new development – official rejection of church before the changes

  — <u>Children's cards</u> - e.g. children making snowmen, playing with snowballs

  — <u>Winter-landscape cards</u> - snowy woods or fields

  — <u>Christmas-tree decorations</u> - typical Bulgarian cards - traditional decorations

他们发现根据图片内容，一共有五类圣诞贺卡：宗教主题的，传统题材的，儿童形象的和冬季景观的，还有一些印了圣诞树的。但是具体的细节并不重要，重要的是他们进行了分类整理。所以学生开始成为研究者了，他们从自己所在的社会收集了数据信息然后进行分析。

接下来学生们开始讨论传统的贺卡和更新的贺卡。一些人注意到，有些贺卡的背面印着"联合国儿童基金会"（UNICEF）的字样，但他们不明白为什么。有的人还发现一些贺卡里印了英语的贺词，虽然这些都是在保加利亚商店里面买的保加利亚贺卡。所以他们就要讨论，到底为什么会出现这样的状况？

每一组必须总结讨论的内容，然后向全班汇报，之后老师会针对英国的圣诞贺卡再做同样的讨论。老师仍然让学生去收集英国的贺卡，并让大家讨论、描述、分类，把这些英国的贺卡和保加利亚的贺卡进行比较。这样他们

about why you buy Christmas cards or why people buy Christmas cards. What do Christmas cards mean to Bulgarians? Who do you send them to? What do you write on them?'

Those questions are the first questions which help them to think about the rules that they follow when they buy Christmas cards. Rules which are not conscious but semi-conscious. They have to try to think about 'Why do I have to do this every year? Who do I send Christmas cards to? Who do I not send Christmas cards to? There are rules which I follow most of the time.' She is asking her pupils to talk in English about what they do as Bulgarians, just as you could ask your learners of Chinese to talk in Chinese about what they do as Americans or as whatever they are.

Then she said, 'Okay, now put your cards into your groups. I want you to decide what kind of cards you have got. You can put them into groups by pictures, or by the writing inside them.'

When they put them into groups, they found five different kinds of Christmas cards by looking at the pictures. They found traditional cards, religious cards, cards with children on them, others with winter pictures on them, and others with Christmas tree decoration. But the details are not important. The important thing is that they began to sort and categorise what they had collected. And so they began to be researchers. They took some data from their society and they began to analyse it.

Then they had to talk in their groups about their traditional cards and the more recent cards. Some of them noticed that some cards, when they turned them over, refer to UNICEF, which is the United Nations International Children's Emergency Fund. And they couldn't understand why that was written on the card. They also noticed that some of the cards had a greeting inside in English, even though these were Bulgarian Christmas cards bought in a Bulgarian shop. So they had to discuss in their groups why, what is happening here?

Each group then had to summarise what they had said, and to report to the whole class. And then the teacher did the whole

- **Third stage**: discussion of the cultural implications: traditional Bulgarian Christmas cards haven't changed; recently introduced innovations, e.g. UNICEF cards with 'Merry Christmas' in English

- *Comparisons*
  – distribute **British cards** to groups: **analyse as before** - four types: religious cards, winter-season cards, children's cards, Christmas decorations.
- – **comparative analysis** of the Bulgarian and British Christmas cards; make two columns: for differences and for similarities; summarise the findings.

- **most striking difference**: information on cards: what **charity** and what material made of

就有了两大类不同的卡片，这些卡片的类别有相似性，但也存在差异。

重要的不是结果，而是过程。学生必须去分析、讨论卡片之间的相似之处和不同之处。其中一个重要的差异就是贺卡上面的信息不同：保加利亚的贺卡上面只印了"联合国儿童基金会"的字样，而英国的贺卡上面却印着很多不同的机构，比如"乐施会"（Oxfam）。老师会说，在英国购买贺卡时，有一小部分钱会捐给慈善机构，这些机构会把钱捐给非洲。所以这是贺卡背后"是什么的知识"。老师发现学生们都很惊讶，因为这一点对他们来说是完全陌生的。1998 年的保加利亚还没有"乐施会"这个机构，所以保加利亚的学生们都感到非常惊讶。他们会讨论英国人为什么要这样做。"在我们的国家我们不会这样做，为什么？因为我们的国家没有穷人。我们不需要把钱捐给慈善机构去救济穷人。因为我们的国家体系会帮助穷人。"但是之后他们又会说道："1998 年，事情又不一样了，我们也是有穷人的。"后来又出现了经济危机，所以他们认为保加利亚也需要发展慈善制度。换句话说，他们开始思考保加利亚的未来应该是什么样子，并积极探索出路。

> ## *Comment*
> - We had a discussion on British charities, their role and value in society. The students learned about some of the well-known British charities - the Samaritans, the Salvation Army, Oxfam, etc.
>
> - They were surprised to find out that these charities got their funds from public donations, not from state or private businesses as is the case in Bulgaria.
>
> - They explained this by reference to the centralised social service system in our country which is still surviving, though quite neglected by the state due to its financial and economic crisis.
>
> - However, they came to the conclusion that the charities in Bulgaria would develop in very much the same way as West European charities because of the guidance they received from them, and the expertise they followed in organisations and activities.

学生们是用英语的思维方式来对保加利亚的情况进行思考的。他们了解了英国的情况，然后把这些知识应用到对其祖国和文化的理解上。在这个过程中，我们谈到了知识（"是什么的知识"），也谈到了技能（"怎么做的知识"），也就是知道怎么去探索、比较和分析。这其中也涉及一些情感因素，比如他们所表现出的诧异。这个活动还涉及批判和评估。学生要思考为什么以前保加利亚没有穷人，但是现在有了呢？在社会主义时期，也就是 1990 年之前，

thing again with some British Christmas cards. She asked students to do the same thing again, discuss them, describe them, classify them, and put them into a comparison with Bulgarian cards. They then had two groups of cards. They had two classifications which were not the identical. Some categories were the same. Some were different.

What is important here is not the result, but the process. They had to analyse. They had to discuss, to talk about what is similar, and what is different. One of the important differences was that the information on the cards was different. The Bulgarian cards talked about UNICEF. The British cards had many other references. They had references to the Salvation Army, Oxfam. These are all organisations like UNICEF, but the teacher told the learners that in Britain when you buy a Christmas card, often a small amount of money goes to a charity, to Oxfam for example which helps people in Africa. So she gave them some information, some 'knowledge that'. And she noticed that they were surprised, because this was strange to them. In Bulgaria, Oxfam in 1998 did not exist; hence they were surprised. They began to talk about why people in Britain did this. 'In our country we don't do this. Why? In our country we don't have poor people. We don't need to give money to the charity to help poor people. Because we have a state system which helps poor people.' But then they began to say that 'In 1998, things are different. There are also poor people.' There was an economic crisis. So they came to the conclusion that charities would develop in Bulgaria too. In other words, they began to reason, to think, and to come to conclusions about what might happen in Bulgaria.

They were thinking in English about Bulgaria, not about Britain or USA or Australia. They learnt something about Britain, and they used that to think about their own country. In other words, they began to see themselves as others see them. In all of this, there are elements which are knowledge, 'knowing that'; others which are skills, 'knowing how' – how to compare, how to discover, and how to analyse. There are also feelings, for example of being surprised. There are also elements which are about being critical and evaluating. They have to think about why in Bulgaria there were in the past no poor people, but today there are. In communist times, before 1990, there were no poor people. Everybody was the same. But today in 1998 and today in 2016, the society has changed. They have to think about why.

In short, they have to learn some languaculture: about the meanings of 'Christmas cards'. But Christmas cards are just a superficial phenomenon. Beneath the surface there are all kinds of beliefs and values. And all of that we can put into

大家都是一样的，所以没有穷人。但是到了 1998 年甚至是当下，社会产生了巨变，他们要思索为什么社会发生了变化。

简而言之，他们要学习一些语言文化：了解"圣诞贺卡"背后的含义。但是，圣诞贺卡只是表层的文化现象，在这个表层之下是各种信念和价值观的汇合。我们把这些总结为一个词，即跨文化交际能力，它同时涉及了技能和知识，即"怎么做的知识"和"是什么的知识"。

谢谢大家！

*　　　　　*　　　　　*

☺ 交流互动

提问人 1：首先，感谢您给我们做了这么精彩的讲座，我非常喜欢，而且我觉得您的讲座非常有意思。您让我们思考一下汉语的情况，我也的确这么做了。您刚才举了英语中摩擦音 th 的例子，问汉语是不是也有这样的发音。汉语有三个发音是很难的：zh、ch、sh，这三个音对国外的汉语学习者而言是非常难的。我也感谢您尊重我们的个体性。我们不想和日本人、韩国人混为一谈。还有一点，您提到有时英国人谈天气会说："今天天气有点冷。"其实这不是在谈天气本身，而是一种问候，正常的反应不是直接谈论天气，而是大概说一下："是的，确实比较冷。"中国人其实也是这样。比如昨天胡文仲教授也举了一个例子。他说在汉语里我们实际上已经不怎么用"吃了吗？"作为问候语了，但我们还是会问"最近忙什么呢？"，尽管我们并不关心你到底打算做什么，这只是一种问候而已。比如有人在玩笔记本电脑，我会说"你在玩儿电脑啊"，这不是问句，而是一种问候。还有一个问题，您提到语言文化这个概念，这是一个合成词，对于汉语教师而言，我不知道课堂语言教学中究竟哪个更重要，是语言教学还是文化教学？谢谢！

one concept of intercultural competence, in which there are skills and there is knowledge. There is 'knowing how' and 'knowing that'.

Thank you for your attention.

*   *   *

☺ Interaction and Communication

Questioner 1: First of all, thank you for giving us this excellent speech. I love it and it's very interesting. You just asked us to think about Chinese, and I was doing that. When you gave me the examples of dental fricative 'th' in English, you asked us if there is any example in Chinese.  These three pronunciations 'zh ch sh' in Chinese are pretty difficult for foreign learners. Sometimes they can be 'the tricky' for learners. And I want to thank you for saying that we are individuals. We don't want to be mixed up with Japanese or South Koreans, because we are Chinese. There is another thing I want to share with you. You said that sometimes when people are saying 'it is cold', actually they are not talking about weather. It is just greeting. The normal reaction is not to talk about the weather directly. We just say 'yeah it is cold' or whatever. The same thing happens in Chinese, too. The example was given yesterday by Professor Hu Wenzhong. He said, actually in Chinese we don't say 'Have you eaten?' as a greeting. Normally we don't say that. But we still do ask whatever you are doing right now and we are not actually asking, 'Are you going to do this or that?'. It is just a greeting. For example, if I see someone is playing his laptop, I can say, 'Oh you are playing with your laptop.' It is not a question. It is just I want to talk with you. And there is another question. As a Chinese teacher, I am not sure in a language class, which one is fundamental? The language study or the culture? That's my question. Thank you.

44

Michael Byram：谢谢你的评论，我也很受益。我觉得这不是语言和文化教学哪个更重要的问题。语言文化这个词是告诉我们，我们既要教语言，也要教文化。语言教学的目的是双重的：我们既要能够使用语言，同时也要能够通过比较你和另一个文化中的人有什么差异来反省自身。你在教学的过程当中，我不太确定中国人是怎么做的，大家可能不送圣诞贺卡，那会送生日贺卡吗？过去如果我们教"圣诞贺卡"这个词，我们就直接去字典里找翻译，学生可以借助字典来进行学习，这就是教学的终点了。现在我们所说的语言文化，不仅是要教如何翻译，或者是说翻译有多难，而是要了解这个词或者是这句话背后的一些文化内涵。所以，我们要学会批判性理解，不仅是要教学生怎么使用语言，同时也要进行自省，对于其他语言文化的人也要进行这样一种评价。因此，思考是非常重要的，只具备使用语言的技能是远远不够的。

提问人 2：您刚才谈到了国家文化的概念，就是由主流群体来定义的文化这一概念。那么美国人在感恩节会聚在一起吃火鸡，所有的美国人都这么做，您认为这是美国国家文化的体现吗？

Michael Byram：是的，大多数美国人在大多数情况下都是这么做的。但是所有的美国人都这样吗？所有美国人每年感恩节都要聚在一起吃火鸡吗？我想并不是这样，总会有一些例外。所以你必须谨慎。的确是有主流群体的。大部分人在大多数时间里都是这样做的。因此当你上课的时候，你的学生说"美国人这么说"，"美国人那么做"，而你想阻止他们的这种过度概括或模式化的成见，你只需说，"让我们来想想中国人吧，是不是有什么事情所有中国人一直都这么做呢？可能也只是大部分中国人通常会这么做吧，因为总会

Michael Byram: Thank you for your comment. Very helpful. I think that it's not a matter of either language or culture. And this word languaculture is an attempt to say we are all teachers of language and culture. The purposes of language teaching are of two kinds: to be able to use language and to be able to think about ourselves by comparing and contrasting what we do and what other people do. In other words, our cultures. So when you teach, I am not sure about Chinese ways of doing things. You probably do not have Christmas cards or maybe you do. Do you have birthday cards? In the past, if you taught the phrase Christmas card and went to the dictionary to find some translations, learners can find a translation in the dictionary. And that is the end. What I am saying by teaching languaculture, is it is not only a matter of teaching how to translate or how difficult it is to translate, but also to understand the meaning behind the words and the sentences that people are learning. By critically understanding, then you are not teaching people only how to use the language, but how to reflect about themselves, about their languaculture and about other people's languaculture. So thinking is important, not just skill in using language, but thinking is important.

Questioner 2: You mentioned the concept of national culture which is defined by the dominant group. So what do you think about the fact that the Americans would get together and eat turkey on the Thanksgiving Day? I believe all Americans would do that. What do you think about that? Is it a national culture?

Michael Byram: Yes. It is something most Americans do most of the time. But do all Americans have Thanksgiving Day and so on? Do all Americans all the time do this? I suspect not. You will always find some exceptions. Always. So in that sense we have to be careful. Yes there is a dominant group. Most of the people most of the time do this. Therefore when you are teaching, if your learners tend to talk about the Americans, 'the Americans do this', 'the Americans say that', and you want to stop them over-generalising, and stereotyping, you just have to say, 'Okay now let's think about the Chinese. Is there something all Chinese all the time do? Maybe there is something most Chinese most of the time do. But there will always be exceptions.' That's important. Remember the phrase 'most people most of the time'. The example of Thanksgiving is a part of a national culture, but I think it is only a surface matter. That's a traditional behaviour. But why do they do that? What are their beliefs behind it? That's more important.

有一些例外。"这一点是非常重要的，大家要记住这个短语："大部分人、大部分时间"。感恩节的确是国家文化的一部分，但我想它只是一个表层问题，一个传统的习俗。人们为什么要遵守这个习俗？他们背后的信念又是什么？这才是更重要的。

提问人 3：刚才教授您谈到"我听到你说的了"这句话，其潜台词是"我对你说的不感兴趣"。我想请教一下，有没有关于文化潜规则的书可以介绍？我觉得对于我们语言教师来说，最大的挑战不是语言知识，而是语言背后的文化潜规则。不知道您是否可以推荐几本书？

Michael Byram：很抱歉，没有这种类型的书。至少我所知道的语言文化类书籍不会告诉你："人们这么说，其潜台词是……"。可能 Kate Fox 那本关于英格兰人的书里会有这样的例子，但是这样的书是很少的。你需要一本能介绍汉语潜台词的书给学生，但没有书会列出所有你该知道的"是什么的知识"，因此很重要的一点是在教学过程中举例子，就像我刚才给大家举的例子，我可以想出几个例子来，把所有应该知道的知识都传授给你，但是我不可能给出各种可能的潜台词；我可以强调技能的重要性，教大家怎么去做，怎么去听，怎么在不同情景中进行判断。如果一位参加英国大学会议的中国老师仔细倾听和观察，就可以看出来，说"我听到你讲的了"的人实际上并没有在听。所以，你要在自己的社会里进行观察，要去听，去想，去思索有意识的、半意识的和无意识的规则，然后学会如何观察这些及其他情况的知识。所以"知道怎么做"要比"知道是什么"更重要。这个问题恐怕没有简单的答案。

提问人 4：我想问一个关于跨文化交际能力的问题。您在 1997 年出版过一本书《跨文化交际能力的教学与评估》，其中提到跨文化交际能力包括语言能力、社会语言能力、话语能力和文化能力，而文化能力又可以进一步分解成五个维度：态度、知识、阐释能力、发现和互动以及批判性的文化意识。刚才您也都讲到了，我想问的是，这五个维度之间有没有什么关系？他们有没有什么共同的基础？能否进一步阐述一下？谢谢。

Questioner 3: Just now the professor said 'I heard what you said', and the implied meaning is 'but I am not interested'. And I'd like to know: are there any books about such cultural norms that Professor Byram could recommend? Speaking from my experience as a language teacher, I feel the biggest challenge is not from language knowledge, but the implicit cultural rules behind the language. Could you recommend some books in this aspect?

Michael Byram: Unfortunately, the short answer is no. At least for English or languages I know or cultures I know, there are no books which will give you 'knowledge that' such as 'Every time somebody says this, they mean something else.' That kind of 'knowledge that' is perhaps a little bit in the book which I mentioned by Kate Fox, but only about the English, and there are so few books like that. Anyway, you need a book for your learners about things in Chinese which they could learn. But there will never be such books. There will not be a book which will give a list of all 'knowledge that' and so it is more important for you to teach learners with examples. As a teacher you say 'I can think of a few examples but I can never give you all the possible knowledge that. I can give you some examples and then emphasise the importance of the skills of knowing how, how to listen, how to see what is happening in that situation.' If a Chinese teacher in a British university meeting listens and observes carefully, he will see that when the person says 'I hear what you say', other people in the meeting realise that he is not listening. So it's a matter of observing and becoming observant in your own society, learning to see what you do. Think about your conscious, semi-conscious and unconscious rules and learn the knowledge how to observe those and other situations. That's why 'knowing how' is ultimately more important than 'knowing that'. So there are no simple answers I am afraid.

Questioner 4: I want to ask a question about intercultural communication competence. In the book, *Teaching and Assessing Intercultural Communicative Competence* published in 1997, intercultural communication competence is composed of linguistic competence and social linguistic competence, discourse competence and cultural competence. And the last one could be further illustrated into five dimensions: attitudes, knowledge, skills of interpreting and skills of discover and interaction and critical culture awareness. As you just talked about, I am wondering: is there a relationship between the five dimensions? And is there a foundation behind these five? Would you please talk about this further? Thank you very much.

Michael Byram：这五者的关系是这样的：

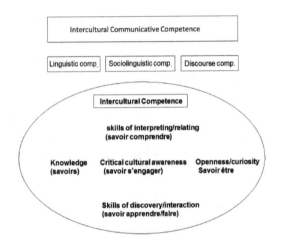

中间的圆圈是技能。是关于怎么做、怎么解读和关联的知识，比如怎么去解读圣诞贺卡，怎么去看它的含义，怎么关联和比较保加利亚和英国的圣诞贺卡。"态度"我之前提得比较少，但是培养学生的态度，尤其是好奇心还是非常重要的。还有发现的能力，就圣诞贺卡的例子而言，学生们要观察别人买圣诞贺卡时的行为，分析圣诞贺卡在本国和在其他国家的不同含义。老师传递给学生的知识是：在英国你买贺卡的时候，大部分人在大部分情况下都是在捐钱给慈善机构。这是"是什么的知识"。

还有其他一些语言能力，是以英语作为工作语言，今天上午我没有谈到，即运用语法的能力、语言能力、得体表达的能力、社会语言学能力、话语能力、与母语者互动的能力。这些能力在学生讨论圣诞贺卡的时候都会涉及。但他们的焦点并不在英语本身上，而是通过英语来思考其他事情。这其实就是学习外语的最佳方法，不是只学"是什么的知识"——当然知识是重要的，但它不能代表一切——而是知道"怎么做的知识"，知道如何运用语言来谈论重要的事情，这是习得语言的方法。但这是需要单独拿出一天时间来阐述的论题。

Michael Byram: The relationship of the five is like this. There are the skills in the middle around the circle. These are the skills knowing how, how to interpret and relate, how to interpret a Christmas card, how to see what it means, and how to relate, compare and contrast it with an English Christmas card. There are also the attitudes which I have not spoken about very much yet. But it is important to develop attitudes in your learners, especially curiosity. The skills of discovery in the Christmas cards example are involved when the students are discovering and observing other people buying Christmas cards, analysing the Christmas cards in their own country and from another country. The knowledge that the teacher gives them is that in England when you buy Christmas cards, most of the people most of the time give some money to a charity. That's 'knowledge that'.

Along the top there are other language competences which come from working in English which I didn't talk about this morning. The ability to use your grammar, linguistic competence, the ability to speak politely, sociolinguistic competence, the discourse competence, and the ability to interact with people in the language. Those are the things which were happening all the time while the students were talking about their Christmas cards. However, they were not focusing upon their language. They were focusing upon other things, but using the foreign language, English in this case. And that's the best way to learn a language. It is not simply to learn the 'knowledge that' about language. It's important but it's not everything. It's 'knowing how' to use a language and to use the language to talk about something important. That's what makes you learn a language. That's how you acquire a language. But that's a different lecture for another day.

课程与课程规划

　　今天的讲座是我和北京语言大学的王丽虹博士一起来做的。丽虹是我多年前的博士生，也是我现在的研究伙伴。

　　我会先给大家举一个基础课程的例子。这个例子是关于西班牙语教学的，但大家即使不懂西班牙语也没关系。之后我会讲一下能力规划的问题。接下来，丽虹会给大家讲一个将文化教材改变为跨文化教材的案例。

举例

　　这是一个关于美国小学的例子，关于 8 岁孩子的西班牙语教学，但其实无论他们是 8 岁还是 18 岁都无关紧要，重要的是他们都是初学者。我已经把课程中的内容都改成了英语，这是美国小学的课堂教学。

Curriculum and Lesson Planning

Today we have a double presentation by Dr Wang Lihong of Beijing Language and Culture University and myself. Lihong was my PhD student a few years ago and we now work together on research.

Let us start with an example from a beginner's course. The example is in Spanish but it doesn't matter even if you don't understand Spanish. Then I will talk about planning by competences. Then, Lihong will give an example of changing a cultural textbook to an intercultural textbook.

> **Overview**
>
> • Example from elementary/beginner language learners
>
> • Planning by competences
>
> • Changing 'cultural' into 'intercultural'

An Example

The example is from an elementary school in the United States, teaching Spanish to children about eight years old, but it is irrelevant whether they are eight or 18 years old; it is important only that they are beginners. I have changed the details into English but originally of course everything was in Spanish, and this is a classroom in an elementary school in the USA.

The students are doing a teaching unit about fruit. They are going to have five lessons of 15 minutes each on this topic. There are language objectives. The teacher wants them to learn some new words

> **The Development of Intercultural Competence in the Elementary School Spanish Classroom**
>
> Michael Byram, Dorie Conlon Perugini, Manuela Wagner
> *Learning Languages Contents* 2013, 18, 1, 16-32

学生们在学习水果这一单元, 共五节课, 每节课用 15 分钟来讨论这一话题。老师希望学生能够学到与水果有关的新词汇、不同水果的表达和一些新的语法知识。老师还设定了语言文化目标。用第一讲的术语来说, 老师希望该目标既兼顾"传统", 又兼顾"现代"。她希望学生知道"是什么的知识", 比如南美洲热带地区西班牙语国家的水果都怎么说, 这是传统意义上的"是什么的知识"。但她也希望学生能够获得一些现代的跨文化交际的"怎么做的知识", 能够比较不同的文化, 从而发现新的"是什么的知识"。这是非常重要的技能, 因为我们不可能什么都教, 也没有书能把学习者想知道的知识全部教给他们。所以学习者必须要学习"怎么做的知识", 以便去发现别人是怎么做的。老师还要问一些问题, 让学生进行批判性思考, 对所学的知识进行反思。同时老师还希望学生有好奇心, 也就是说, 通过上这门课学生能够对他人的行为感兴趣。尽管这门课只涉及吃水果这一个方面, 但老师希望学生们能借此对饮食文化这个话题产生兴趣。总之, 老师希望学生能够了解"是什么的知识"和"怎么做的知识", 正如我在第一讲中提到的, 这两者结合在一起, 就是一种跨文化交际的能力。

> 'Fruits from around the World' Unit
> [5 lessons (15 minutes)]
>
> Language objectives: 'fruit' vocabulary and new grammar
> Languaculture objectives
> Traditional ['cultural'] → knowledge that : information about tropical fruit
> Modern [Intercultural] → knowledge how:
>   – To compare 'our' eating culture with 'theirs'
>   – To discover new knowledge about what people **do**
>   – To ask questions – critical cultural awareness
>   – To become curious [about other people's eating culture – what they **do**]
> • AND KNOWLEDGE THAT… = COMPETENCE

新的知识包括关于水果的新词和新的语法结构。他们将学习如何用西班牙语来说: "你最喜欢的食物是什么"、"你最不喜欢的食物是什么"。学生会用到一些他们已知的西班牙语词汇和语法。比如他们已经知道怎么用西班牙语表达"多少", 然后把这些已知的词汇和语法同新学的内容结合起来进行语言练习。这些就是这位老师经常做的事情。

但是, 学生不仅要彼此问"你最喜欢什么水果, 最不喜欢什么水果", 因为实际上, 他们八成已经知道其他同学最喜欢的水果是什么了。所以这些都不是实际的问题。我们需要要把这种练习性的问题变成真实的问题, 只有

for fruit, different kinds of fruit, and some new grammar. She also has some languaculture objectives. She wants her objectives to be both 'traditional' and 'modern' to use the terms from my first lecture. She wants them to learn some 'knowledge that', concerning fruit in tropical Spanish speaking countries in South America. That's the traditional 'knowing that'. But she also wants them to learn some modern intercultural 'knowledge how'; how to compare, and how to discover new 'knowledge that', about what people do. This is a very important skill because we cannot teach everything, and there are no books which tell learners everything they might want to know. So they have to learn the 'knowledge how', to discover for themselves about what people do. The teacher also wants to teach them some questions which will begin to make them think critically, to think about what they are learning critically. In addition to this, she wants them to become curious. She wants to have a lesson which will stimulate their curiosity about what other people do. In this case, it is a small example about eating fruit, and she wants to stimulate their curiosity about this topic. In short, she wants them to have some 'knowledge how' and some 'knowledge that', and the two together are what makes 'competence', as I said in the first lecture.

That new knowledge includes learning new vocabulary for fruit, and new grammar structures. They will learn to say in Spanish 'What is your favourite? What is your least favourite?' To do this, they will use some words which they know already in Spanish, and some known grammar. They already know how to say in Spanish 'how many' for example, and are going to combine some known words and grammar with some new, and practice their language. All of this is what this teacher always does.

However, they are not just going to practice their language by asking each other: 'What is your favourite fruit? What is your least favourite fruit?' because in fact they probably know what is the favourite fruit of their friends in the classroom. Those are not real questions; they are just practice questions. We need to make their practice questions into real questions and this will happen when they go out into the rest of school to meet other children they do not know, and ask them about their favourite fruit. Then they are also

Learn and Practice Vocabulary and Grammar
• New words for 'fruit'
• New grammar: 'What is your favourite... / least favourite...'
• Old/ known words: 'popular'
• Old / known grammar: 'How many?'
• PRACTICE = DO A SURVEY IN SCHOOL – DO SIMPLE STATISTICS

当他们进到别的班级，问那些他们并不熟悉的人时这些问题才能生效。他们还应该走出学校，进入他们所在的社区、大街小巷和他人的家庭之中，问一些真实的问题，即答案未知的问题。

然后他们可以做一些简单的数据统计。他们可以计算有多少人喜欢这种水果，又有多少人喜欢那种水果，等等。

老师会以非常传统的方式引入新词汇：给他们一些图片，问他们图片中的物体应该怎么表示。这只是普通的语言教学法。

然后老师会和学生一起做问卷，当然是西班牙语问卷，但这里我译成了英语。

他们会使用已知的词汇和语法，还会用新学的语法（"how many"）和关于"水果"的新词汇造句。随后老师会让学生回到家里用西班牙语向朋友和邻居提问。在他们的社区，有很多人会说西班牙语，所以他们可以用西班牙语问问题。如果他们的朋友不会说西班牙语，可以用英语来问，但是要把答案翻译成西班牙语。

下面开始统计数据。这些都是真实的数据，学生们会像社会学家一样展开调查，观察、收集并分析数据，就吃水果这个问题而言，总结出"大多数人在大多数时间"的习惯。

然后老师会制作一个谷歌地图，把收集到的信息在地图上呈现出来。大家可以看到地图上有很多点，点击后就会展示出一些信息。教师可以在计算机房授课，让学生探索地图背后的信息，了解有多少人吃、吃多少种水果，等等。在这里非常重要的一点是语言要非常简单，学生们通过提问来分析大多数人在大多数时间是怎么做的。老师必须要避免过度概括和思维定式，不能让学生以为所有的西班牙人都爱吃橘子，而是应该让学生认识到"大多数西班牙人在大多数时间"爱吃橘子。

- Next step - pupils survey people from other countries in local community - in English but reported in Spanish

- Spanish teacher creates Google Map showing which fruits most and least popular in different countries.

- Pupils have one lesson to explore the map in the computer lab.

- To avoid over-generalising/stereotyping, teacher discusses 'sample size' in Spanish - students have already been familiar from maths lesson.
  - e.g. teacher points to one pin on the Google map and asks in Spanish 'How many people does this pin represent? Does it represent the entire country? Would the answer be the same or different if we ask every person in the country?'

going to go out into their community, into the streets around, into their friends' and families' homes, and are going to ask real questions, i.e. questions where they do not know the answers.

Then they will do some simple statistics.

Questionnaire questions (translated)

- What is your favourite food?
- What is your least favourite fruit?
- What is the most popular fruit in the United States?
- What is the most popular fruit in Spain?
- How many pieces of fruit do you eat in a day?
- How many pieces of fruit should you eat in a day?
- How many pieces of fruit do our friends eat in a day
- How many pieces of fruit do your parents eat in a day?

Adding up how many people like this, how many people like that, and so on.

The teacher introduces all the new vocabulary. She does that in a very ordinary way – showing them pictures, asking 'what is the word for this [object in the picture], what is the word for that?'. That's all just ordinary language teaching.

Then together they make a questionnaire. It's in Spanish of course, but I have given the English translation.

They use vocabulary and grammar which they know already, and then the new grammar 'how many?' and the new words that they know for fruit. Then the teacher asks them to go home, and ask their friends and neighbours these questions in Spanish. In their local community, there are quite a few people who speak Spanish. So they can ask their questions in Spanish, or they can ask them in English and change the answers into Spanish.

They begin to do statistics; this is real data, and they are beginning to act as social scientists. They observe, collect and analyse data, learning how to analyse what 'most of the people most of the time do', in terms of eating fruit.

Then the teacher created a google map, and put the information that they had collected onto the map. When they click on the points, they can see some information. Then the teacher allows them a lesson in the computer lab. They explore the map and do some simple statistics. How many people eat, how many fruits, and so on. The important point is this is simple language, and they are asking questions to find out what most of the people most of the time do. The teacher has to avoid overgeneralisation and stereotype. She doesn't want them to think that all people in Spain always eat oranges. She wants them to think 'most people most of the time' eat oranges.

To do this she points to the map, and asks them in Spanish how many people this pin represents. Each of the pins or points on the map represents some information. 'Does it represent the entire country? Would the answer be the same

为了达到这一目的，老师会指着地图，用西班牙语问大家，这一个点代表多少人。地图上每一个点都代表一些信息。老师指着这个点说："这个点能代表整个国家吗？如果我们问这个国家里的每一个人，答案会是一样的吗？"当然每一次的答案都不一样，只能说明大多数人大多数时间会做出这样的选择。

换句话说，老师将传统语言教学和现代语言教学融合在一起。她给学生提供了一些"是什么的知识"，同时也教学生**如何**来了解西班牙语者的生活习惯，并且与自身的习惯进行比较。这个专题的另一节课是讨论水果的价格，在此我不详述了。他们还会问这样的问题，如这个水果多少钱？他们的母亲总是买同一种水果吗？还是说在大部分情况下会买？在不同的时节这种水果会不会更贵？这种水果产自哪里？他们的父母是在过去吃热带水果多一些还是现在多一些?

Traditional [Cultural] and Modern [Intercultural]

- Knowledge:
    - Traditional: Knowledge about local fruit and tropical fruit
    - Modern: eating habits of 'us' and 'them'; cost of fruit; fruit and climate; availability of tropical fruit has changed from parents to children generation; AND not all questions can be answered
- Skills of interpreting and relating
    - Traditional: ----
    - Modern: comparing fruit eating norms in own and other groups

---

这个问题背后牵扯到了全球经济的问题，老师应该引导学生对此展开讨论。鉴于这个问题比较复杂，大家可能既会用到英语又会用到西班牙语。不是所有的问题都有答案，但关键要让学生开始思考，要**批判性**地思考——为什么现代人比过去吃水果多？为什么过去人们不吃热带水果，现在会吃？老师应该决定在西班牙语课堂中主要使用哪种语言。老师应该考虑是不是应该只留 10% 的时间让学生用英语来讨论，或者是留 20% 的时间？老师必须要做出恰当的选择，确定分配多少时间说英语是适当的。

除此之外还有知识技能（Byram，1997）的学习，即如何进行**阐释**。传统教学只是教"是什么的知识"，在这里，学生则要学会**如何对比和比较**。他们要了解人们在自己的群体和在其他国家或群体时的饮食习惯，通过提问了解**"如何去发现"**。传统教学就是在课上进行词汇和语法训练，而他们所

or different if we ask every person in the country?' And of course the answer each time is 'no'; it's only most people most of the time.

In other words, the teacher is doing some traditional language teaching and some modern language teaching. She is giving some 'knowledge that', but in some modern ways, she is teaching them *how* to learn 'their' habits compare with 'us', as the children compare and contrast what they do with what Spanish speaking people do. They also, in other parts of the lesson which I won't discuss in detail now, talk about the costs of the fruit, dealing with questions such as 'How much does it cost? Does their mother buy the same fruit all the time or some of the time? Is it more expensive at different times? Where does it come from? Do their parents eat more tropical fruit now or in the past?'

Behind this lies the idea that we are now in a global economy, which the teacher encourages the learners to discuss. This is partly in Spanish and partly in English, because some of these things are quite complicated. There are not answers to all of these questions but the important thing is to make the learners begin to think and think *critically* about why people eat now more fruit than they did in the past, why they eat tropical fruit, which in the past maybe they didn't eat, and so on. The teacher has then to decide which language to use in the Spanish classroom. Is it just 10 percent of the time that she will give the learners time to discuss in English? Or is it 20 percent? The teacher has to decide if it's appropriate and how much time they can use English.

There are then skills (Byram, 1997) of knowing how to *interpret*. Traditionally, we only taught 'knowledge that', but here they are learning *how to compare and contrast*. How people eat in their own group and in other countries and other groups, and they learn *how to discover* this for themselves by asking questions. Traditionally, learners practised their words and their grammar in the classroom, and the information, and the content of what they were saying, were not important. They already knew the answers to their questions; it was just practice. Now, the learners carry out their survey and they ask real questions. They go out into the

表达的内容和传达的信息并不是很重要，因为他们已经知道问题的答案了，只是在练习而已。现在他们要展开调查，问出真实的问题。他们会去学校向陌生的学生提出这些真实的问题。

老师还要激发学生的**好奇心**，通过分配任务培养学习兴趣。传统课堂是不会进行这种设计的，因为传统教学的重点就是语言。而现代教学中学生会充满好奇心——我们是怎样吃水果的？其他人又是怎么吃水果的？我们所在的社区、村庄或小镇，可能有不同的习惯。有的人比较爱吃水果，有的人不爱吃水果，所以要避免过度归纳，要让学生保持好奇心。

- Skills of discovery and interaction:
    - Traditional: learners ask each other questions to practice words and grammar
    - Modern: learners carry out survey – ask people outside school – real questions
- Attitudes of curiosity
    - Traditional: not the focus – lessons focus on language
    - Modern: learners curious about norms of fruit eating of 'us' and 'them' but also variation within 'our' community

当然，还要有**文化思辨意识**。传统教学是没有这个环节的，但是现代的老师会让学生进行批判性思考，从而考虑到这样的事实：即使我们的国家不生产热带水果，我们也可以全年都吃到热带水果。全球化让我们全年都能够吃到美国进口的热带水果。但这是好事吗？还是有什么问题？有没有环境上的代价？老师应该提出这些问题让大家思考。

以上涉及的关键词——文化思辨意识、学习发现和比较的能力、学会保持好奇心——这些都是课程规划能力的基础。

基于能力的课程规划

能力是一种混合物，它既包含"是什么的知识"又包含"怎么做的知识"。所以老师在规划课程的时候应该思考，"我希望学生们掌握怎样的技能？我希望他们知道什么？"或者换种说法，"在教完这节课或这个单元之后，我的学生会'知道是什么'"。这些传统的教学方式非常重要，但并不是全部。"学生将知道是什么"的不仅是语言知识，还包括文化和语言文化方面的知识。

school to other children
they don't know, and ask
real questions.

The teacher also tries
to build up *curiosity*. She
tries to make them curious
by giving them things to do.
In traditional lessons, she

> • Critical cultural awareness:
> – Traditional: ----
> – Modern: questioning costs of fruit; questioning the environmental cost
>   of having fruit all year

did not do that, because all the focus was upon language. In a modern lesson, the
learners become curious about what is 'normal' when 'we' eat fruit and when 'other'
people eat fruit, whether in other countries or within our community or within
our village or within our bit of the town. There are different ways of doing things.
Some people eat a lot. Some people eat a little. So to avoid over-generalisation, the
teacher tries to make them curious.

Then there is *critical culture awareness*. It is not part of traditional language
teaching but now the teacher begins to make her learners think critically about the
fact that we all eat tropical fruit all the year, even though it's not produced in our
country. Globalisation has allowed us to eat tropical fruit in the United States all
year. Is that a good thing? Is that problematic? These are the questions that she gets
the learners to think about. The environmental cost of all this.

The key words mentioned above – critical cultural awareness, learning how to
discover, learning how to compare, learning to be curious – lie behind the lessons
which have been planned by competences.

Planning by Competences

Competence is a mixture, a combination of 'knowing that' and 'knowing how'.
So when you plan your lessons, you need to think 'What do I want my learners to
be able to do (know how), and what will I want them to know (know that)?' Or to
put in other words: 'By the end of this lesson or this unit, this group of lessons, my
learners will 'know that...' That's the traditional aspect of teaching, important but
not everything. 'They will know that' refers to language but also to culture and to
languaculture. 'Secondly, by the end of the lesson, the learners will know how... [to
do certain things]'. They will know how to use the language, but they will also know
how to compare and contrast.

Let's look at this in more detail. There are three kinds of objectives: language
objectives (linguistic grammatical objectives), communicative objectives (how to

其次，在课程结束后，学生应该"知道怎么做"。他们将知道怎样使用语言，也将学会如何进行对比和比较。

Planning [and assessing] by competences

- Reminder: competence = knowing that + knowing how

- Planning:
- By the end, learners will know that…
- By the end, learners will know how…

具体而言，我们在进行课程规划的时候有三类目标：语言目标（语法目标）；交际目标（即如何礼貌和得体地使用语言）；跨文化目标。第一类目标是传统的教学目标，大家都很熟悉了。第二类我们可能也比较熟悉。第三类跨文化目标则是新的理念。

应该说在我们规划课程时，大部分课程或单元（或是教材，不过这一部分王丽虹一会儿会讲到）都涉及这三类目标：

－语言／语法的目标：在课程或单元结束后，学生应该"知道是什么"，比如英语里面第三人称单数的谓语动词要加 s。或者学汉语的话，他们要"知道"汉语里面的动词没有时态的变化。但他们也要学会"怎么做"，即如何使用英语里的第三人称单数来造句，如何用副词而不是动词变形来表示汉语的时态等。所以一节课或系列课程结束之后，他们既要"知道是什么"又要"知道怎么做"。

－交际目标：课程结束后，学生应该"知道"哪些表达方式是礼貌的，而且他们也要"知道如何"得体地**使用**语言。比如，怎么运用汉语口语去描述他们的假期，也需要知道怎么用正式的书面语和上司进行口头或文字交流。所以他们既需要掌握知识本身，也要学会区分汉语不同的礼貌用语，在其他的语种里亦然。这就是交际目的。

－跨文化目标：课程结束之后，学生们要知道怎么进行对比和解读，无论是圣诞贺卡还是水果的例子，都是在教学生**对比和解读**"他者"和"自身"。而在你们的教学活动中，这个"他者"指的是中国人，"自身"指的则是美国人、越南人、英国人或其他国家的人。他们应该学会**解读**发生在中国的事情——

use the language politely, appropriately), and there are intercultural objectives. The first are traditional and we are all familiar with those. The second kind of objective is probably familiar as well. The third kind is what is new.

> 3 kinds of objectives for planning :
> 1) linguistic/grammatical,
> 2) communicative [appropriate/ polite],
> 3) intercultural
>
> (most) lessons [and textbooks] should include (3) objectives which are:
>
> • Linguistic /grammatical: by the end of this (series of) lesson learners will
>
> > • know that (e.g. (for English as FL) 3ʳᵈ person singular takes 's')
> > • CHINESE EXAMPLE
> > > • THERE IS NO MARKER OF TENSE IN VERBS – BUT USE ADVERBS
> >
> > • know how to produce *written* English in which the 3ʳᵈ person singular 's' is accurate
> > • CHINESE: BE ABLE TO PRODUCE REFERENCE TO THE PAST AND FUTURE

In order to use this way of thinking, we should say when planning lessons that in most lessons or groups of lessons (and textbooks – but I am talking about lessons, Lihong will talk about textbooks later), there should be three kinds of objectives:

- linguistic/grammatical objectives: By the end of this lesson or series of lessons, learners will 'know that'. For example, in English, the third person singular takes 's'. Or if they are learning Chinese, they will 'know that' there are no tense markers in Chinese. But they will also 'know how', for example, how to produce in English with a third person 's'; they will know how to speak Chinese referring to the past and the future and the present but not using the verb, using the adverbs. So they will 'know that' and they will 'know how', by the end of this lesson or series of lessons.

- communicative objectives: By the end of this lesson or series of lessons, the learners will 'know that' certain kinds of ways of speaking are polite. And they will 'know how' to *use* language appropriately. So they will know, for example, how to use colloquial Chinese to talk about their holidays. They will know how to use formal Chinese to talk or to write to their boss. So they will know how and know that there are different kinds of politeness in Chinese as in every other language. Those are communicative objectives.

- intercultural objectives: By the end of the lessons or series of lessons, they will know how to compare and contrast, to interpret, to take Christmas cards or fruit or whatever, and

> ## Communicative = appropriate language
>
> • communicative: by the end of this (series of) lesson learners will
>
> > • know that (e.g. the use of colloquial expressions is acceptable among friends but not with teachers),
> >
> > • and know how to talk about their holidays in two styles, colloquial and formal

比如中国人吃什么，又或者更大的问题，比如中国人的宗教信仰等。他们要学会**发现**，要提出关于中国文化的问题，从而获得新的知识。他们将在真实的情景中学会这些。所以在课程结束时，我的学生应该能问出任意话题的问题。

NOW ADD INTERCULTURAL COMPETENCES
'know how'

By the end... know how to
Skills of interpreting and relating: ability to
• interpret a document or event from another culture (Chinese), to explain it and relate it to documents or events from one's own

Skills of discovery and interaction: ability to
• acquire new knowledge of a (Chinese) culture and cultural practices
• Read, ask questions, etc. to find out...
• and the ability to operate knowledge, attitudes and skills under the constraints of real-time communication and interaction.
• Ability to mediate/explain (an aspect of) Chinese culture to a friend...

他们也能够成为**交际媒介**，能够向其他人讲述有关中国的话题。不是讲述全部的中国文化，即所有中国人都会做或应该知道的事情，而是作为美国人、越南人或任何一个国家的人的媒介来解释有关中国的话题。

最后，他们还要有评估的能力，要能够进行批判性思考，清楚地进行评价。为什么我要这么看中国？为什么我要这么看自己的国家？我所使用的标准是什么？举个例子，我认为学生具备了评判好与坏的能力，但衡量"好"和"坏"的标准是什么呢？"好"意味着我是赞许的，如果我说什么东西是好的，这本身不能说明什么，只能说我对此是表示赞许的。而更重要的是，为什么我要赞许它，为什么我觉得有些东西是好的。比如儒家思想中的孝道和长幼尊卑的概念，我知道这些概念很复杂，在这里我只能简明扼要地说一下。假设一个学习汉语的美国人学到了"孝"的概念，即要遵从你的父亲。他们会认为"这很对啊！"或者"这可不对！"。但这只是第一步，作为教师你还应该让他们去思考："为什么会这么想？"。再比如，在美国，人们非常强调友谊的概念，尤其是社交媒体中"朋友"的概念。这些都被看作是好的，这个现象背后是人们对朋友或友谊等概念的认同，因此可以和中国的孝道进行比较。学习汉语的美国人可能会想，"我们的做法对，但听从父命我并不赞成，或无法理解。"作为教师，你就要问他们，"你为什么这么想？你是怎么想的？你觉得在你们的文化里会怎么做？为什么你们的文化会觉得友谊很好但遵从长辈并不见得好？"

compare and contrast 'them' and 'us'. And in your case, for your learners, 'them' is the Chinese, and 'us' is the Americans or the Vietnamese or the British whoever the learners are. They are able to *interpret* an event from China – it might be what people eat in China, or it might be a much bigger issue about what people believe, about religions or whatever. They will be able to *discover* for themselves. They will be able to ask questions, to ask people about things in Chinese culture, and thus acquire new knowledge for themselves. They will be able to do that in real time. By the end of this lesson, my learners will be able to ask questions about whatever.

And they will be able to *mediate*. They will be able to explain to other people about something in China. Something simple. We are not talking about all Chinese culture. We are not talking about everything Chinese people do or know. And they will be able to mediate or explain that to other Americans or other Vietnamese or wherever they come from.

Finally, they will have the ability to evaluate to think critically and be clear about their evaluation. Why do I think about this about China? Why do I think about this about my own country? What are the criteria that I am using? I might for example think that the learners will be able to evaluate good and bad behaviour. What do I mean by good and bad? 'Good' means it is something I approve of. If I say something is good, that means nothing. It only means I approve of it. The more important thing is why do I approve of something. Why do I think something is good. For example, take the concept of filial obedience or obedience to authority in Confucius thinking. I know it's complicated and I simplify. An American, learning Chinese, learns this notion of filial obedience, obedience to your father. They think 'That's good! Or that's bad!'. But that is only the first step. The teacher must get them to think 'Why do I think like that?', or take something from American or British culture. In the US, there is a lot of emphasis upon the notion of friendship, not least in the social media where people have 'friends'. And this is thought of as good. Beneath that phenomenon, there are some values about friends, and friendship, which can be compared and contrasted with Chinese values of filial obedience. The American learner of Chinese might think, 'Yeah what we do is good, and obedience to father, that's not something I approve of, or that's something which I don't understand'. The question teachers have to ask them is why they think in this way. 'What is your thinking? What is in your way of doing things in your culture which makes you think that somehow friends is a good thing, and obedience to older people is not such a good thing?'

Those examples are of knowing how to interpret, knowing how to compare and contrast, knowing how to discover for yourself, and knowing how to be critical.

Add: 'Critical cultural awareness'

- By the end... know how
- **Critical cultural awareness:** an ability to evaluate, critically and **on the basis of explicit criteria**, perspectives, practices and products [OR values, beliefs and behaviours] in one's own and other cultures and countries
  - Evaluate 'good' and 'bad' behaviours/values/beliefs, e.g. 'filial obedience' in China; emphasis on friendship and social media in USA

这些例子就是要让学生知道如何去解读、比较和对比，要知道怎么进行自主的探索和批判性思考。

与此同时，老师也要给予学生一些"是什么的知识"。因为中国老师确实对中国很了解，积累了很多关于中国的知识，但并不是完全的中国通。老师可以为学生提供一些自身掌握的知识，但不管老师教给学生怎样的知识，这些知识都只是"大部分人在大部分时间会做的事"。而且传授知识也只是你作为教师的一部分职责而已，更重要的是教学生如何应用这些知识（怎么做的知识）。

总而言之，很多目标在课程规划的过程中都至关重要，在评估的过程中也是举足轻重的，这个问题我们会在之后的讲座中详谈。

现在我们来谈谈教材。我知道大家所使用的汉语课本和其他课本没什么两样，都是传统的教材，讲授关于中国的知识。当我在学校教法语的时候，课本讲的是关于法国的知识，我们要做的就是把传统的"文化"教材（因为它能提供"是什么的知识"）变成"跨文化"的教材，在这里重要的是进行比较和对比，不仅要探索我们自己的国家和中国，而且还要批判性地分析我们所探索到的内容。

这一部分将由王丽虹为大家讲解。

从"文化"到"跨文化"的课本改编

王丽虹：

首先我想要感谢 Mike 邀请我来到这里，非常高兴能见到大家，非常欢迎各位汉语教师。我是十年前读的博士，Mike 今天邀请我，并不是因为我是他的学生，而是因为我在美国乔治·梅森大学的孔子学院工作，和那里的

At the same time the teacher is also responsible for giving some 'knowledge that' because of course teachers do have knowledge. Chinese teachers have some knowledge about China, maybe a lot of

> Add: 'KNOW THAT'
>
> • By the end... know that:
>   • 'in China, most people most of the time...':
>   • EXAMPLE: eat fruit a lot; believe fruit is healthy; value fresh fruit rather than preserved fruit
>   • OR WHATEVER YOU THINK IS APPROPRIATE

knowledge, but they don't know everything about China. Teachers have some knowledge and can give that knowledge. Whatever it is the teacher tells learners, it has to be about 'most of the people most of the time'. But it's only part of what you do as a teacher. It's more important to teach learners the skills, the knowing how.

To sum up, there are different kinds of objectives which are crucial for planning but they are also useful in assessment as we shall see in a later lecture.

We now turn to textbooks. We know that textbooks for teaching Chinese, like textbooks everywhere, are 'traditional' in the sense that they give knowledge about China. In my textbooks when I was a school teacher, it was knowledge about France. What we have to do is to use those textbooks which I call traditional and 'cultural', because they give 'knowledge that', and change them into 'intercultural' textbooks, where the important thing is that we emphasise comparing and contrasting, discovering about our own country and about China, and critically analysing what we find.

This is the part which Lihong will do.

Changing Textbooks from 'Cultural' to 'Intercultural'

Wang Lihong:

First of all, I'd like to say: thank Mike for inviting me to be here. Let me explain why he has done so. During the last five years, I have been working at Confucius Institute at George Mason University in the United States, and I have been working closely with Chinese teachers. I know what they have been through and how they resist the changes of teaching beliefs and how they construct their new professional identity as an international Chinese language teacher in a kind of culture context zone.

I'll start talking in Chinese in this section. (Note: The Chinese can be seen on the previous pages in the Chinese part. Here they are translated into English.)

In fact, I have looked at many textbooks of Teaching Chinese to the Speakers

汉语教师密切合作。我知道他们的经历，知道他们是如何在某一文化背景下抵制教学理念的变革，如何作为国际汉语教师建构新的职业身份。

这一节我会用汉语来讲。

我其实看了很多中国出版的对外汉语教学的书，发现很多书的共同特点是既教汉语语言，也教中国文化。我随便拿了一本北京大学出版社出版的《汉语口语速成》，这也是我们北京语言大学汉语速成学院普遍使用的教材。我随便挑了一课，比如"做客"，这一课里面讲到中国人的饮食文化，讲外国学生到中国人家做客，整个对话我就不读了，其实在座的各位国际汉语教师可能非常清楚，我的感觉是，我们是在教一个外国人怎么成为一个中国人。教材中的学生大卫说的话都是中国人教他说的，比如"不早了，我该回去了"，"给你们添麻烦了"。这样的话可能会从日本学生、韩国学生的嘴里说出来，但是欧美学生不习惯这样说话。所以，我们在编写教材的时候，要考虑是从什么样的视角编写教材，是从文化的视角、中国文化的视角，还是跨文化交际的视角。以前澳大利亚的学者也说，所有澳大利亚的汉语教科书，第一课的第一句话都是"欢迎到北京来"。澳大利亚的学生应该说"欢迎到澳大利亚来"，美国学生应该说"欢迎到美国来"，这些都是最基本的原则。

那么，我们应该教什么样的文化呢？我们在孔子学院工作的时候，的确有很多关于中国文化的资源。我们现在教文化，可能很大程度上是教一些事实上的文化，一些介绍性的内容，也就是 Mike 刚才用到的一个词——declarative knowledge（陈述性知识）。比如在文化教学中，我们选择了最基本的就餐文化和饮食文化，除了语言目的，这本书还谈到可能使用的一些词和短语，像"筷子"、"礼物"、"一双"、"一副"以及"还"的句式，比如："还拿什么礼物"，相当于"不要拿什么礼物"，这是中国主人经常说的一句话，表示客气。还有怎么表现得很有礼貌，了解中国人就餐的文化和一些常识，这都是拓展知识，在教科书里面都没有谈到。教师可能让学生根据实际情况介绍自己国家的就餐情况，这在我们的教案中没有明确地写出来，但老师可能在课堂上挖掘到这一方面。

所以，从跨文化的角度，我们需要对不同文化中的就餐文化进行比较，让学生能够发现这些规则背后的一些文化理念，能够提出一些问题来展示其文化思辨意识，从而对他国文化更感兴趣。因此，兴趣也是可以教出来的。

of Other Languages which are published in China, and they share a lot in common, that is, teaching Chinese language and Chinese culture. I pick up one for *Short-Term Spoken Chinese*, which is published by Peking University Press and used as the textbook in the College of Intensive Chinese Training of Beijing Language and Culture University. I select one lesson on 'Being a guest'. I'm not going to read the dialogue part, but I guess that the Chinese language teachers here may be quite clear that in this text we are teaching a foreigner to become a Chinese. In this dialogue, we Chinese put the words and sentences into the mouth of the student, David, such as 'It is getting late, and it's about time for me to leave now; Sorry for all the troubles/bother'. All these sentences may sound natural if spoken by the students from Japan and South Korea, but the students from European countries and America may not be used to this way of speaking. So, when we are compiling textbooks, we need to consider the question that in what perspective we are doing this, from the perspective of culture, i.e. Chinese culture, or in the intercultural perspective. I once heard an Australian scholar said about the textbook used in Australia. Almost all the first lessons in the textbooks start with 'Welcome to Beijing'. To the Australian students, it should be 'Welcome to Australia', and to the American students, it should be 'Welcome to the US'. This is the very basic issue.

Then, what culture we teach? When I was working at the Confucius Institute, we have loads of Chinese cultural resources available. To much extent, the culture we are teaching is factual culture, an introduction to culture knowledge, which is termed by Prof. Michael Byram as 'declarative knowledge'. In teaching culture, for instance, if we choose to teach eating culture or food culture, besides language terms, such as 'chopsticks', 'gifts', 'a pair of' , and the language structure '*hai...*' which means 'no need do...', an expression often used by Chinese to show their consideration and politeness. We also teach manners to make students understand Chinese eating culture and cultural common senses, which is a kind of extension, for these aspects are not explicitly presented in the textbook. The teacher may ask the students to introduce the eating culture of their own countries, trying to explore the issues with the students; however, these are not explicitly included in the lessons.

So, from intercultural perspective, we need make comparisons between different eating cultures, to make the students discover the cultural beliefs behind those rules. They can ask questions to show their critical cultural awareness, so as to get more interested in other cultures. Here we say that curiosity can be taught as well. All these competences and skills are teachable. Let's take 'using chopsticks' as an example. Chinese use chopsticks to eat their meals. In Mike's words, 'Most

上述所有能力和技能都是可以教的。我举一个最简单的例子，比如讲到筷子的时候，中国人是用筷子吃饭的，用 Mike 的话说，"大部分的中国人，大部分时间是用筷子吃饭的"。但我们自己的文化也是有差异性和多样性的。首先，我们可以让学生做一些调查，如"谁使用筷子？"，甚至一家人吃不同的食物也会使用不同的餐具。如果把它变成一个带有跨文化维度的例子，那就让学生来做这方面的调查，除了中国人以外，是不是其他民族也使用筷子？筷子是怎么使用的，正确使用筷子的技能也是学生需要掌握的。中国人的就餐文化中有很多禁忌，包括筷子的摆放或者筷子的使用方式。让学生做一个调查，收集数据并在课堂上展示。

最后要有一个比较和反思的步骤。学生肯定说，不光是中国人使用筷子，其他东亚民族也使用筷子。即使都使用筷子，但是筷子也是不一样的；可以启发学生发现有什么不同。日本的筷子、韩国的筷子是什么样的；中国的筷子是什么样的；他们在长度、形状和质地上都是不一样的，那又是为什么呢？这些都是启发学生思考的问题。我在美国乔治·梅森大学孔子学院工作的时候，学生对孔子学院汉语教师的各种评价分数都特别高，但是其中有一项"引发思考"，中国教师的分数都低于院系和大学的平均水平，因为美国大学并不那么重视知识的传输，而是注重智力和认知能力的开发。老师们可能会辩解，"我就是教基础汉语的，怎么可能在课堂里融入高层次认知能力？"其实美国从小学甚至是幼儿园到初中的 K-12 教学体系都会融入思辨能力的教学，而大多数汉语教师缺乏这方面的技能，这也是 Michael Byram 教授在最后一张幻灯片里要讲到的问题。

这些图片显示的是筷子的使用和禁忌，一目了然，我们就不细讲了。中国人摆放筷子时不能把筷子插在饭碗里，学生肯定会问为什么。我们怎么解释，从而让他也可以去跟别人解释？我们在培养学生的时候，不只是说让他知道"是什么"或者"怎么做"，而是使他成为文化的中介，能够在两种文化间进行对比和比较，能够向本国人解释中国人为什么这样做，也能从中国人的角度分析问题。我们不期待学生能够成为中国人，而是希望他成为具有跨文化意识的交际者。

刚才我说了，就"发现和互动"而言，传统的教科书只是教你"做什么和不做什么"，而我们要培养学生的思考能力和认知能力，即让学生发现和

Chinese most of time use chopsticks to eat their meals'. Even in our own culture, we have variations and diversities. We can ask students to do research on the topic 'who is using chopsticks?' Even in one family, family members may use different tableware to have different types of food. If we extend it into intercultural dimension, then, ask students to do some research to find out besides Chinese people, are there any other nation uses chopsticks as well? Besides, the proper use of chopsticks is also the skill that the students need acquire. Chinese have many rules and taboos regarding the proper use of chopsticks, such as the placement of the chopsticks on the table, the manners of using chopsticks. Ask the students to do a survey and collect and bring the data to the class to present.

Lastly, we should have a section for comparison and reflection. The students surely find out that not only Chinese use chopsticks, people from other eastern Asian countries use chopsticks, too. However, even if they all use chopsticks, the chopsticks are not all the same. We can encourage students to discover differences in the chopsticks used by Japanese, South Koreans and Chinese, in terms of length, shape, and materials and try to find out why there are such differences. All these questions are intended to inspire the students to engage in thinking. When I was working at the Confucius Institute of George Mason University, our Chinese teachers receive high scores in most of the indicators from the students' evaluation, but only on one item 'The class is intellectually stimulating" our Chinese language teachers' scores are below the average of both the department and the university, since American universities put less emphasis on knowledge transmission and more on thinking and developing students' intellectual and cognitive abilities. Our Chinese teachers would argue by saying 'we are only teaching basic Chinese, how can we teach high-level cognitive thinking skills in class?' In fact, critical thinking skills are integrated into the teaching in the K-12 schools, even in kindergartens in the US. Most of Chinese teachers lack these kinds of skills. Professor Mike Byram will talk about this in his last slide.

These pictures show the taboos and use about chopsticks. You all know well, so we won't talk about this in details. Chopsticks should not be put into the rice bowl, and your students surely ask 'why not?' How do we answer such questions so that the students could explain this practice to others? When we are cultivating a student, we are not just teaching him knowledge or behaviour; we are developing him into a cultural mediator, who is able to make comparison and contrast between cultures, who can explain to his own people why Chinese behave in this way, and can look at things from Chinese perspective. We do not expect him to become a Chinese, but hope that he can become a person with intercultural competence, that

解释中国的筷子为什么长，日本的筷子为什么通常短而尖？老师给出的答案永远不是标准的答案，学生可以通过调查来寻找答案。比如这可能是和日本人喜欢吃鱼有关，头是尖的更好用一些。中国的筷子甚至有一个具体的长度，应该是多长？七寸六分（大概八英寸），据说代表了人的七情六欲，这也只是知识层面的。中国人的筷子长，也可能是因为中国人通常围着圆桌吃饭，所以筷子要长一点；日本人的筷子短，可能因为他们的食物通常离得比较近，因此筷子不需要那么长。韩国的筷子为什么是扁的？可能因为是妻子把食物递给丈夫，所以圆的筷子容易滚落，扁的比较容易夹住。无论如何，类似的知识都是来自他人的，不是学生自己的，所以我们需要帮助学生把知识转化成自身的能力。如果学生的好奇心被激发出来，他们可能会问，"在首尔的中餐馆用什么样的筷子，用金属的还是木头的？谁能回答？"这个时候要鼓励学生在现实生活中使用和检验知识，比如去中国人居住的社区。美国的外语教育遵循几个原则，称为5C原则，其中一个C就是"community"（社区），就是让学生学以致用，比如到中餐馆真正去体验。

谈到怎样培养学生的文化批判意识，即让学生通过学习语言成为世界公民或通过语言教育成为跨文化公民，学生必须具备一些基本的意识。这是传统教学的短板。现在我们可以引导学生讨论一次性筷子的使用。我们可以质疑一次性筷子的发明。一次性筷子是日本人发明的。日本人每年要消耗250亿双筷子，每个人一年大概消费200双筷子。日本的筷子并不是用本国的木材生产的，99%是进口的，其中96%来自中国。事实上，中国的森林覆盖率只有14%，而日本却是65%。日本人知道如何保护本国的资源，而不是浪费。

学生可以进一步探讨使用一次性筷子的危害。如果一次性木质筷子对环境有危害，他们可以采取行动不用一次性筷子。在你的课堂，你可以决定把百分之多少的课堂时间分配给学生用母语，谈一些与其智力和认知能力相匹配的深层次的思想。

刚才我们谈到课堂语言教学的目标，即交际得体性。课文中，主人会说"还拿什么东西啊？"，学生至少需要理解，虽然它是一个问题，但表达的不是问题，听上去像是抱怨，但却不是。这个语言现象本身已经凝聚了中国文化的部分内容。具备跨文化能力的学生，不光了解中国的就餐文化以及如何使用筷子，而且可以从这些文化器物和行为习俗中，阐释中国人是如何看待

is, an intercultural speaker.

Just now I said that in 'discovery and interaction', traditional textbooks only teach 'do's and don'ts' , but we need foster students' thinking and cognitive abilities, that is to say, we should ask students to discover and explain why chopsticks are longer in China, why the chopsticks in Japan are usually shorter and pointed? The answers the teacher provide are not always the correct answers, and the students seek the answer through their investigation. For example, it is because Japanese love eating fish, and pointed chopsticks are more helpful. We know Chinese chopsticks even have a specified length. How long are they? It said 7'6" (about 8 inches). Representing human beings' seven emotions and six desires – this is also only on the level of knowledge. And that Chinese chopsticks are longer may be because we usually sit around a round table, long chopsticks are more suitable; Japanese chopsticks are shorter, which may be because their food are severed relatively near them, long chopsticks are not necessary. Why South Korean chopsticks' heads are not round but flat? Maybe because when the wife serves food for her husband, it is easier for the flat ones to hold still, for the round ones will easily fall. Anyway, all these knowledge is from others, not the students' own, so we need help students to turn knowledge into their own competence. If students' curiosity is fostered, they may ask the question like 'What the chopsticks are like in the Chinese restaurant in Seoul, metal ones or of wood? Who can answer?' Here we can encourage students to use and test their knowledge in reality: to go to the Chinese community. In the US, foreign language teaching follows the 5C principle, among which there is 'community', which means the students need use their language in their real life, for example, go to the Chinese restaurant to have authentic experience.

Then how to foster students' critical cultural awareness? That is to say, we make students become world citizens or intercultural citizens through language education, then the students must acquire some basic awareness. Traditional language education falls short in this respect. Now we can lead the students into the discussion about the use of disposable chopsticks. We can question the invention of disposable chopsticks. Disposable chopsticks were invented in Japan. Japanese use 25 billion pairs of chopsticks each year – about 200 pairs per person. 99% of the wood used for producing chopsticks is imported, and, in fact, among which 96% is imported from China. As a matter of fact, forestation in China is only 14%, as compared with 65% forestation in Japan. They know how to protect their own resources and not to waste them.

The students can further explore the negative effects of using disposable chopsticks. If disposable chopsticks are not environmentally friendly, then they

这个世界的。因此学生可能会问，中国人为什么会有这么多餐桌上的规矩，这是我们要讲给学生的，使得他们能向别人介绍。

然后他们就能够从中国人的视角来理解为什么中国人把吃看得这么重要。你也可以让学生去查查字典，看看里面带有"吃"字的汉语词汇是不是明显比其他民族多。中国人说"吃香"，"吃亏"，还可以"吃官司"，这样的表达在其他语言里面都没有，也侧面反映出语言是文化的载体，一个文化最重要的东西肯定在其语言当中都有体现。

从这个层面，我们也可以引导学生以一种思辨的视角看待中国文化中的"客气"、中国人的人情味和中国人的面子，也就是培养学生文化思辨意识。Mike 用到 critical cultural awareness 这个表达，这是外语教育中非常重要的层面。我想和大家分享的就是这些。重要的是，我们不能使中国文化程式化。中国人的饮食习惯和餐桌礼仪不断变化，各家有各家的饮食习惯，我们在麦当劳里也不用筷子吃饭，而是用手吃饭，不是吗？

An example of changing a 'cultural' textbook unit/chapter into an 'intercultural' one

Change the Lesson planning so that learners have to

(1) compare with their own country,
(2) find out some new information about the topic in their own country and in China and compare,
(3) critically analyse what they find.

Lived culture (food culture, eating culture)

教学目的：

Language objectives: 学会运用本课所学词语："筷子"、"礼物"、语法："一双"、"一副"及句式："（还）V. 什么（＊＊）呀"（表示否定，意为"别／不用 V."）

Languaculture objectives：

◆ 让学生掌握去中国人家里做客和主人待客的得体表达方式和习惯；
◆ 了解关于中国人就餐的常识和文化；
◆ 熟练运用本课所学词语、句式，根据实际情况介绍自己国家的做客和就餐习惯·
　　• To compare Chinese eating culture with your own eating culture
　　• To discover new knowledge about what people **do**
　　• To ask questions – critical cultural awareness
　　• To become curious [about other people's eating culture – what they **do**]

themselves can take action not to use them. In your language class, you can decide on how much time you allow your students to use their mother tongue to talk about their deep thoughts, which match their intellectual and cognitive development.

We've talked about the goal of language classroom: appropriateness is the goal for communication. In the text, the host said 'how come you bring stuff?', the students need to understand at least that this sounds like a question, but it is not a question; it sounds like a complaint, but it is not either. This language phenomenon has embodied some aspects of Chinese culture. The students with intercultural competence not only know Chinese culture in dining and using chopsticks, but from these cultural products and practices, they can also interpret and explain how Chinese people view the world. So, the students would ask why Chinese people have so many rules at dining table, and we need to make them understand so that they could explain these practices to others.

Then they could understand from the Chinese perspective why Chinese view eating as such an important thing. You can also ask the students to look up in the dictionary to see if terms with the word/morpheme

> 'eating at a Chinese home' Unit
> [2 lessons (2 hours)]
>
> • Language objectives: vocabulary and new grammar "其实"、"V.什么 (O.) 呀"!
> • Languaculture objectives
>   • Traditional → knowledge that : information about 'eating' culture
>   • Modem [ICLT] → knowledge how:
>   • To compare 'our' eating culture with 'theirs'
>   • To discover new knowledge about what people do
>   • To ask questions – critical cultural awareness
>   • To become curious [about other people's eating culture – what they do]
>   • AND KNOWLEDGE THAT... = COMPETENCE

'eat' are much more than those in other languages. So that many expressions in Chinese with 'eat' as a component provide evidence that language is the vehicle reflecting its culture. An important cultural event must be presented in its language.

From here, we can encourage the students to view Chinese culture of 'being polite', Chinese relationship and reciprocity, and Chinese 'face value', with a critical attitude. We need to foster the student's critical attitude towards cultures. Professor Michael Byram terms it 'a critical cultural awareness'. This is a very important aspect in foreign language education. I think that is all about my presentation. Importantly, we should not stylise Chinese culture. Chinese dining habits and table manners are changing all the time. Each family has their own dining habits and rules. We don't use chopsticks at McDonald, do we?

Task-based PBL learning

Pre-task:
- Who use chopsticks? (Map)
- How are chopsticks used? (Youtube video clip) Any taboos?
- When are chopsticks used?

During-task:
- Students present findings to each other

Post-task:
- Evaluate

Culture and Communication

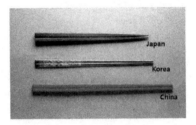

similarities and differences

- Critical cultural awareness:
  - Traditional: ----
  - Modern: questioning the invention of 'throw-away' chopsticks; questioning environmental cost of manufacturing chopstics a year.

  日本：25 billion pairs/year, about 200 pairs/per person, per year
       96% from China, (日本，森林覆盖率 65%；中国，森林覆盖率 14%)

  根据学生的水平，讨论一次性筷子的危害：
  - ➢ 随意丢弃，影响市容环境
  - ➢ 砍伐树木，浪费资源，破坏环境
  - ➢ 化学处理，不卫生，影响健康

Planning [and assessing] by competences

• Reminder: competence = knowing that + knowing how

• Planning :
• By the end, learners will know that...
• By the end, learners will know how...

---

3 kinds of objectives for planning :
1) linguistic/grammatical,
2) communicative [appropriate/ polite],
3) intercultural

(most) lessons [and textbooks] should include (3) objectives which are:

• Linguistic /grammatical: by the end of this (series of) lesson learners will

  • know that ("过"，表示过去：“吃过”、“听说”、“看过”；量词使用 measure words “一双筷子”)

  • know how to

Communicative = appropriate language

• communicative: by the end of this (series of) lesson learners will

  • know that (e.g. the use of 客气 expressions，“还拿什么东西呀”)，

  • and know how to （使用客气或习惯表达方式，“不早了，我该……了。）

NOW ADD INTERCULTURAL COMPETENCES
'know how'

By the end... know how to
Skills of interpreting and relating: ability to
- interpret a document or event from another culture (Chinese), to explain it and relate it to documents or events from one's own
- 中国筷子的标准长度是七寸六分，代表人有七情六欲；餐桌用餐礼仪和禁忌；
- **Skills of discovery and interaction:** ability to
- acquire new knowledge of a (Chinese) culture and cultural practices
  - Read, ask questions etc. to find out...
  - 为什么中国人在餐桌上有这么多规矩？
- and the ability to operate knowledge, attitudes and skills under the constraints of real-time communication and interaction.
  - Ability to mediate/explain (an aspect of) Chinese culture to a friend...
  - 能够从中国人的角度来解释"吃"的重要性

Add: 'Critical cultural awareness'

- By the end ... know how
- **Critical cultural awareness:** an ability to evaluate, critically and *on the basis of explicit criteria*, perspectives, practices and products [OR values, beliefs and behaviours] in one's own and other cultures and countries
  - Evaluate 'good' and 'bad' behaviours/values/beliefs e.g. 客气、人情味、面子 in China; emphasis on friendship and social media in USA

Michael Byram:

希望这些例子能帮助大家思考汉语教学中的问题。我想最后再强调一下"知道怎么做"的重要性。当然，"是什么的知识"仍旧是传统教学内容。在现代教学中，我们要让学生在"知道是什么"的同时掌握"怎么做"的技能。

The story so far – the framework

- 2 kinds of knowledge AND we should teach both = 'competence'
- Culture = values, beliefs and behaviours [rules/conventions] shared by most but not all in a group (from small to large, from family to nation)
- Culture and language are connected = LANGUACULTURE
- We can specify which competences to teach
- The teacher has a dilemma...

*   *   *

Add: 'KNOW THAT'

- **By the end... know that:**
  - 'In China, most people most of the time...':
  - EXAMPLE: eat with chopsticks, but not always, for example, in McDonald; belief in taboos; value appropriate dining behaviours, 客气，面子;
  - OR WHATEVER YOU THINK IS APPROPRIATE
    - The process of producing throw-away chopsticks/plastic forks and knives – not good for health;
    - environmental issues

Objectives for lessons

intercultural: by the end of this (series of) lesson(s), learners **will know** that stereotypes are never true (for example: fortune cookies) OR **know that chopsticks are not only used in China;**

will know how to identify and **critically analyse** stereotypes in a text (in the target language) about their own country and about China.

OR know how to **discover** for themselves stereotypes about their country held in country X [or discover more about origins of chopsticks, forks, knife, and throw-away chopsticks]
（中国人的用餐规矩也在不断变化，不是每个家庭都尊重传统，各家有各家的规矩和习惯）

AND/OR be able to/know how to **compare and contrast** documents and perspectives in own and China, e.g. stereotypes about China in their own country and stereotypes of own country in China [or compare dining/giving gifts with similar occasions in their own country]

Michael Byram:

I hope the examples have helped you to think about the teaching of Chinese. Let me emphasise in conclusion the importance of 'knowing how'. Of course 'knowing that' is still a part of what we do traditionally. In a modern way of teaching, we have to 'know that' and have the skills of 'knowing how'.

- Teaching by objectives = By the end, learners will know that... and learners will know to...
- 3 kinds of objectives: linguistic, communicative, intercultural
- Textbooks are 'cultural' and teach 'knowing that' – we need to change them into 'intercultural' = comparison, discovery, critical analysis and 'real' language use

---

*　　　　　*　　　　　*

☺ 交流互动

提问人1：如果我说跨文化交际是一种解放或颠覆，您是否会赞同？在学习外语或是第二语言的过程中，学习者的身份也发生了变化。他们不再处于一个比较低的地位，而是站在了较为中立甚至是更高的地位。在跨文化课程设置中，把传统的语法课程或是语言、交际方法融会贯通好像要相对容易一些。事实果真如此吗？我很想听听您的看法。

Michael Byram：你说的没错。学习者的身份的确改变了。传统意义上，当我们在教语言和语言能力时，这种改变是隐性的。学习者要做的就是模仿母语者。从语言的角度来看，即模仿母语者的语法知识以及"知道是什么"和"知道怎么做"。这是语言能力的问题，而且至今仍然悬而未决——学习者是否应该模仿母语者？从文化能力和跨文化能力的角度来看，这种模仿实际上是不妥当的。我们希望学生通过将自己置于他者和自我之间来建立一种新的身份，这种从中沟通的能力、阐释与解读的能力是不同于模仿者的身份的。

但对于学习者来说，仍有一些方面需要模仿母语者，比如语法知识和语法的准确使用。但大部分情况下，即便是关于礼貌的问题，我们也要以一种不同的身份来思考。像丽虹刚才提到的，有些东西是可以模仿母语者的，比如礼貌用语的使用。但问题是，是不是总是像中国人那样讲话就很得体呢？假如美国的汉语学生模仿中国人是否合适？有时候合适，有时候就不合适。所以，解放思想的意思是说学习者可以有两种选择，要么站在跨文化的角度，

成为两种文化的中间人，要么去模仿母语者。但这是需要学生自己来选择的，老师已经有够多的问题和困境了，不必为学生决定一切。

提问人2：教授您好。您的讲座给我留下

☺ Interaction and Communication

Questioner 1: Would you agree if I say that intercultural approach is liberating or subversive? Because it's in the process of learning a foreign language or second language that the identity of the learner has changed, that is, the learners no longer position themselves in a lower status but it seems that they have acquired a more neutral or higher status. In the intercultural curriculum, it seems that it can be relatively easy to integrate the traditional grammatical curriculum or linguistic curriculum or communicative approach. Is that so? I would appreciate any thoughts you would like to share.

Michael Byram: You are right. The identity of learners changes. Traditionally, when we were teaching language and language competence, the change was implicit. The idea was that our learners should imitate native speakers. And in language terms therefore they had to imitate the grammatical knowledge and the skill of 'knowing how' and 'knowing that' of a native speaker. That is a question in language competence. That's still an open question, i.e. whether imitating native speakers is appropriate, but in terms of cultural competence or intercultural competence, the idea of imitating a native speaker is not appropriate. We are trying to develop in our learners a new identity which comes from this idea of mediation or being able to put yourself between the other and yourself. That mediation competence, of being able to explain and interpret, is a different identity to the idea of imitating a native speaker.

There are still some things in which it is important to imitate a native speaker for example, with respect to grammar and grammatical accuracy, but in most things we have to think in terms of a different identity even with respect to politeness. As Lihong said, there are some things in which you can learn to imitate a native speaker, for example, with respect to politeness. But the question is: Is it always appropriate to act as if you were a Chinese? Is it appropriate for your American learners of Chinese to imitate Chinese? Sometimes it is, sometimes it isn't. The liberating notion is that they have the two possibilities of sometimes being mediators or adopting a kind of intercultural position, and sometimes trying to imitate. But these are the things the learners have to decide for themselves, not the teacher. The teacher has enough dilemmas, enough problems without having to decide everything for the learner.

Questioner 2: Hello professor. I'm very impressed by your lecture. As you say,

了深刻的印象。正如您所说，不同国家有不同的文化。作为汉语老师，有些情况是我们没有遇到过的，但作为老师我们必须要做出回应。比如，我有一个韩国学生，他总是在宿舍里待着，不愿意去教室上课。我就问他为什么。他告诉我，之前当兵的时候太累了，所以他现在需要放松，需要休息一段时间。大学生活对他来说就是用来放松的。而我跟他说，你应该刻苦学习，可这么说对他没什么效果。所以我的问题就是，除了成绩和惩罚措施，有没有什么办法能够鼓励这样的学生走出寝室？在不同国家的学生进入我们的大学之前，我们是否应该针对不同的国情准备好相应的教育措施呢？谢谢。

Michael Byram：如果我没有理解错的话，这是另一类问题，关于学生的身份及自我认知。传统意义上的老师无所不知，老师将知识传授给学生。但我们现在要做的是让学生更能够为自己的学习负责。培养独立的学习者我们都已经耳熟能详了，这也是非常重要的。如果我对您的问题理解正确的话，那么我就可以这么说，学生思维的变化是缓慢而循序渐进的。老师仍然是权威，但并不是全知全能的。老师是"权威"，但不具有"权威性"。这两个词对于我们进行翻译的朋友来说可能比较难区分。其实，老师是帮助学生去学习的，他是一个促进者。但老师并不是万事通，没有办法把自己所掌握的知识全部转移到学生的头脑中去。学生要学会如何学习。这个过程会十分缓慢，因为大部分时间里，学生都习惯从老师那里学习知识，将老师视为知识的唯一来源。这是一个漫长的过程，需要一定的时间。

王丽虹：我想说中国学生的学习动机比较强，他们比较喜欢学习。从我在美国五年的工作经历来看，并不是所有学生到你的课堂里面都有学习动机，或者想把汉语学好。在美国，老师需要激发并且保持学生的学习兴趣，这是非常重要的。另一方面，我经常说，中国老师自带权威（authority is institutionalised），然而在美国你需要使你的课堂非常吸引学生（engaging the students），让学生喜欢这个课堂是非常重要的。

所以，这也是为什么我们要在语言课堂里融入学生的经历和他们的文化背景。他可能说我对中国并不感兴趣，学汉语只是为了获得通识教育（liberal education）的学分，有时只是想体验一下，更不用说是主修或辅修汉语了。

different country has a different culture. As a mandarin teacher, there are some situations we have not encountered but we need to react because we are teachers. For example, one of my students is from South Korea. He often keeps himself in the dorm and never enters the classroom. I asked him why. He told me that he was too tired when he was in the army. And now he needs to relax. The university time is his relaxing time. I told him that you need to study hard. But it's ineffective for him. So my question is that except grade and punishment, do you have some proper ways to persuade him to go out of his dorm? Do we need to prepare some different measures according to different countries of students before they come to the university? Thank you.

Michael Byram: In a sense, this is another question about learners' identity, and what learners think about themselves, if I understood you properly. Traditionally the teacher knows everything. The teacher transfers their knowledge to their learners. But I think what we are now trying to do is to make learners more responsible for their learning. The independence of the learner is one of the phrases that one hears a lot. I think it's important. If I understand your question correctly, the change in the learners' thinking will be slow and gradual. The teacher is still an authority, but he does not know everything. The teacher is an authority but is not authoritative. That might be a difficult distinction for my friends in the translation booth. The teacher is an authority who helps the learners to learn. But he or she does not know everything, and is not trying to transfer what is in his or her head into the heads of the learners. The learners have to learn how to learn. That's a slow process. For most of their lives, learners have been expected to acquire knowledge from their teachers and see the teacher as an only possible authority. It's a slow process which will take time.

Lihong: I'll say in China the students coming to the class are motivated to study well. They like to learn. Speaking from my five years of working experiences in the US, I feel that not all the students who come to our class are motivated and aiming at studying Chinese well. It is the teacher's job to motivate the students to learn and to protect their curiosity for learning. This is very important. Another thing about this is that in China, the teacher's authority is institutionalised, while in the US, you have to make your class very engaging, and make your students like your class. This is also an important thing.

That is also why we should integrate students' experiences and their cultures into the classroom. The student may say that I am not interested in Chinese things;

我们要知道学生的期待和他们想学什么，而不是单方面考虑我们想教什么，所以学习是要协商的。

提问人3：我也有一个问题，教授能不能介绍一下跨文化交际与欧洲流行的交际型教学法之间有什么联系？

Michael Byram：我觉得交际型语言教学是在传统教学的模式上加入了新的内容，除了强调"是什么的知识"和"怎么做的知识"之外，还应该知道如何得体或礼貌地运用语言。这就是交际型语言教学对传统语言教学的补充——其强调的是礼貌得体和口语技能，而传统的语言教学更强调的是写作技能。这种从传统的教学模式到交际型教学模式的转变早在三四十年，甚至是五十年前就已经在欧洲和北美兴起了。这种转变就是从"是什么的知识"转向"怎么做的知识"，从强调写作转向强调口语，从简单使用语言转向得体礼貌地使用语言，这些就是从传统到交际型教学的主要转变，但并没有改变学习者需要模仿母语者的观点。在交际型教学法中，学习者会在有意无意的状况下模仿母语者。但是从交际型教学到跨文化教学的转变，强调的是我们之前说过的学习者的身份问题，他不是去模仿母语者，而是要成为一个中间人，一个不同文化间的斡旋者，而不是一个地道的母语者。这就需要不同的技能和不同的思维方式了。在某种程度上，用简单的短语或一两个词来概括的话，语言学习者要成为一个民族志学者，一个人类学家，他要去了解另一种文化中的人，能够进行对比和比较，能够进行批判性地分析。我们曾经写过一本书叫做《作为民族志学者的语言学习者》。这个书名基本涵盖了我们想要做的一切。

王丽虹：我建议你读一下 Mike 2008 年的著作《从外语教育到跨文化公民教育》。它可以回答您刚才提到的从交际教学法到跨文化教学模式转变的问题。因为我们的目标不同，所以教学方法也就不一样了。

he learns Chinese just for the credits required for liberal education; sometimes just for experience, to say nothing of majoring in Chinese or taking Chinese as a minor. We should know what the student expects, and what he or she wants to learn; not just what we want to teach. So learning needs negotiating.

Questioner 3: I also have a question. Could you tell us is there any relationship between intercultural communicative approach and communicative Language teaching approach popular in Europe?

Michael Byram: I think communicative language teaching added something new to traditional language teaching by emphasising that in addition to knowing about and knowing how to use language, we also need to know how to use language appropriately or if you like politely. That is the extra that communicative language teaching added to traditional language teaching. Because it added this emphasis upon politeness and appropriateness, it also at the same time emphasise much more the speaking skills, whereas in traditional language teaching, the emphasis was upon writing skills. All of this happened 30, 40 almost 50 years ago in Europe and North America, i.e. the change from traditional to communicative, from 'knowing that' to 'knowing how', from writing to speaking, and from simply using language to using language politely and appropriately. That I think is the big shift from traditional to communicative. The shift from traditional to communicative still did not change the idea that the learners should imitate the native speakers. In communicative language teaching, learners were implicitly, sometimes explicitly, learning to imitate the native speakers. The move from communicative to intercultural is to emphasise the point that was made a moment ago that the identity of the learner is not to imitate the speaker but to become something in between, an intercultural speaker, a mediator, someone who is not a native speaker. And that requires different skills, and different ways of thinking. In a way, and this is another little phrase, to capture everything in one or two words, the language learner becomes an ethnographer, an anthropologist, i.e. people who think about how to learn about other people, compare and contrast and critically analyse. One of our books is called *Language Learners as Ethnographers*. That little phrase captures everything that we are trying to do.

Lihong: I suggest you read Mike's *From Foreign Language Education to Intercultural Citizenship Education* (2008), which will answer your questions about the transformation from communicative language teaching approach to intercultural approach. Since we have different goals, then we adopt different approaches.

评价与评估

回顾第一讲和第二讲的主题

在谈评价之前，我想我们有必要先总结一下我们讲过的内容。在讲座的框架中涉及两种知识，并且这两种知识是我们在教学中都应该教授的，即"是什么的知识"和"怎么做的知识"。这两种知识结合起来就是能力。

其次是如何定义"文化"的问题。我讲到"文化是一个动词"。换句话说，文化指我们的**行为**。文化即我们做了什么。在行为的背后则是我们的**价值观**——我们认为重要的东西，以及**信念**——我们所信仰的真理。所以，文化首先是一系列的规则或传统。但它又不像语法规则或法律规则那样固定，而是一种常规，就是"大多数人在大多数时间怎么做"。任何一个群体都有它的文化，像一个家庭这样的小群体有自己的文化，行业群体有自己的文化，而更大的群体，比如国家，通过教育和媒体也能够塑造出民族归属感。因此国家就是一个"想象共同体"，你不可能认识这个群体里的每一个人，只能"想象"我们属于同一个群体。这个群体越大，这种想象的属性也就越强，也就是说不可能形成一个"体验性"群体，即人们互相都很熟悉。我们隶属各种各样的群体，既有体验性群体也有想象性群体。

Assessment and Evaluation

Review of Themes from Lecture 1 and Lecture 2

Before I begin to talk about assessment, I think it will be useful to summarise where we are so far. The framework is that there are two kinds of knowledge and we should teach both kinds of knowledge, both 'knowledge that' and 'knowledge how'. Together those two make up the idea of competence.

Secondly, there is a question about what we mean by 'culture'. I used the phrase 'Culture is a verb'. In other words there are *behaviours*. Culture is what we do. Behind those behaviours are the *values*, what we think is important, and *beliefs*, what we believe in, the ideas that we think are true. Culture is then first a matter of rules or conventions. Not rules like grammar rules which are fixed, like laws, but conventions, what 'most people most of the time' do. Most but not all, in any group, whether it's a small group like a family – a family has a culture, or a large group like a profession – a profession has a culture, and even a larger group like the nation, which through education, and through the media creates a sense that we all belong together in a certain nation. That is an 'imagined community' because we cannot know everybody in the group or community – we 'imagine' our belonging together with them. The bigger the group, the more it is an imagined group, not an 'experienced' group, i.e. one where we can know everyone. We belong to many different groups, both experienced and imagined.

The third point is that language and culture are connected. We experience our life through language, so we experience our culture through language. This means that we are not just language teachers, we are languaculture teachers. We teach language and culture together.

The fourth point is that on the basis of what has just been said, we can now start to *plan our teaching*. It's important to plan by specifying the competences, the knowledge how, the knowledge that, which we want our learners to acquire. We need to specify our objectives and outcomes for the end of our lessons, a point I will come to in a moment.

Fifth, it is important to realise that when we become language and culture

第三，语言和文化是相互联系的。我们通过语言来体验生活，也通过语言来体验文化。这就意味着我们不只是语言教师，更是语言文化教师，我们要同时教授语言和文化。

第四，我们现在可以在以上概念的基础上进行**教学规划**了。在规划的过程中，重要的是要明确学生需要学习哪些能力，"怎么做的知识"以及"是什么的知识"。所以我们要明确在课程结束时需要达到怎样的教学目标以及教学效果。这一点我一会儿还会谈到。

第五，必须意识到，作为语言文化老师，我们并不是中立的。在教学过程中会涉及价值观和信仰问题，这就意味着老师经常面临一种**困境**：老师应该在多大程度上鼓励学生接受或是认同某种价值观、行为或理念？如果你是一位汉语老师，又是中国人，那么你所面临的困境就是，你希望自己的学生在多大程度上认同中国的文化，或者是你希望不管他们有多了解中国文化，也仍然与中国文化保持一定的距离。这个问题我一会儿也会谈到。

现在我们再回到规划的问题上来。我们应该通过制定**教学目标**来进行教学规划，也就是说要明确在一节课或一系列的教学之后，学生应该学会"是什么的知识"，掌握"怎么做的知识"。一共有三种目标。我们都知道的是语言目标，"下课时，我的学生应该学会……（关于汉语的某些知识）。下课时，我的学生应该会（用汉语）表达……"。除此之外，还有交际目标，"通过这节课或这门课，我的学生能够了解汉语里的礼貌用语使用规则，知道如何得体地、礼貌地运用汉语"。这也是实现第三个目标——即跨文化目标的第一步，"上完这节课或这门课之后，我的学生能够知道……（关于中国文化的一些内容），能够解读、比较、对比和挖掘中国文化的内涵"。这些都是新的理念：让学习者学会对比和比较本国文化和中国文化，自主探索中国文化的内涵，并通过对比和比较，对本国文化和中国文化进行批判性分析。之后，我也会详细谈一下批判性分析的问题。

最后，王丽虹提到了教材，教材也是有"文化性"的，因为教材常常聚焦于"是什么的知识"。这很重要，但是还远远不够。所以，王丽虹也谈到了如何把"是什么的知识"转变成"怎么做的知识"，就是要在你的课本中加入比较和探索的维度，这样就可以使学生和课本读者掌握不同类型的"怎么做的知识"：知道怎样进行比较、探索和批判性地分析。这就是王丽虹强

teachers or languaculture teachers, then this is not a neutral activity. It involves values and beliefs. This means the teacher has a *dilemma*: To what extent should the teacher encourage their learners to identify with certain values, behaviours and beliefs? As teachers of Chinese who are themselves Chinese, the dilemma is to what extent you want your learners to identify with Chinese culture, or to what extent you want them to understand Chinese culture but nonetheless to remain distant from it. I will talk more about this later.

Let me return to the question of planning. We need to plan by *objectives*, by what the learners will know, will 'know that' and what the learners will 'know how', by the end of a lesson or a series of lessons. There are three kinds of objectives. The ones which we all know: the linguistic objectives. 'By the end of this lesson, my learners will know that... (something about Chinese language). By the end of this lesson, my learners will know how to say... (something in Chinese).' Then there are communicative objectives. 'By the end of this lesson or series of lessons, my learners will have knowledge about politeness rules in Chinese and know how to use Chinese language appropriately and politely.' And that is the first link towards the third kind of objective: intercultural. 'By the end of this lesson or lessons, my learners will know that... (something about Chinese culture) and my learners will know how to interpret, compare, contrast, and discover things about Chinese culture.' Those are the new ideas: the importance of your learners' acquiring knowledge how to compare and contrast their own culture with Chinese culture, and to discover more about Chinese culture for themselves, and to make critical analysis by comparison, critical analysis of their own culture as well as of Chinese culture. And I will say more about critical analysis later.

Finally, Lihong talked about textbooks and how textbooks are 'cultural' in the sense that they usually focus on 'knowledge that'. That's important but it's not enough, and then Lihong began to talk about how to change 'knowledge that' into 'knowledge how', or to add to your textbooks a comparative and discovery dimension, which will allow your learners and readers of the textbook to acquire those different kinds of knowledge how: knowing how to compare and discover and analyse critically. Thus Lihong emphasised the importance of changing a 'cultural' textbook into an 'intercultural' textbook. I know there are textbooks which are already intercultural, which are already introducing into the textbook the 'know how', not only the 'know that', but many textbooks we use are still 'know that'. We need to improve them.

调的要点，即从"文化"的教材变成"跨文化"的教材。我知道有很多教材已经是跨文化的了，已经在"是什么的知识"的基础上引入了"怎么做的知识"，但是我们用的很多教材还是只教授"是什么的知识"。我们需要对此加以改进。

举例：在母语国家的母语教学

前两讲中我给大家举的例子都是语言教师在其他国家里教授自己的母语：在保加利亚教英语，在美国教西班牙语等。关于如何在中国教外国人汉语的问题，我们需要再举其他的例子。例子更能够揭示问题，也更为重要。这个是来自丹麦的例子，丹麦语老师在本国向外国人教授丹麦语。就像汉语是中国的官方语言，而丹麦语是丹麦的官方语言。

'Why do Danes put their elderly in nursing homes?'
Working outside the classroom with adult second language learners
Judith Parsons and Peter Junge (Denmark)

From: Byram, Nichols and Stevens (eds) 2001 *Developing Intercultural Competence in Practice*. Multilingual Matters

在这个案例中，学习者实际上都是生活在丹麦的移民或是寻求庇护者，他们已经是成年人了。这些学习者可能不是汉语课堂上的学生，但是就像大家在中国教汉语一样，这些学生也是在丹麦本土学习丹麦语的。21个成年人组成了一个班，其中有8名女生和13名男生，年龄不等，国籍各异，有的来自阿富汗，有的来自伊拉克，还有一些来自索马里、黎巴嫩、斯里兰卡、泰国、罗马尼亚、土耳其等国家。他们从这些国家移民而来或是寻求政治庇护。

在课堂上，学生们已经充满了好奇。有时候我们需要激发学生的好奇心，但是在这个例子中，学生们已经对老一辈丹麦人的生活充满了好奇。他们想知道，丹麦人是如何对待老年人的？他们之所以感到疑惑，是因为通过对日常生活的观察，他们觉得丹麦人好像对他们的父母或长辈的关心程度比不上阿富汗、伊拉克、斯里兰卡这些国家。他们非常关心的是，丹麦老年人过得怎么样。

所以老师就设计了教学目标。到课程结束时，学生应该了解其本国老年

An example from teaching a language in the country where it is spoken

I want to give you another example because my examples in the first two lectures were from people teaching their languages in another country: English in Bulgaria, or Spanish in the United States. For those teaching Chinese as a

> Language classes in Danish as L2 for migrants/asylum-seekers
>
> 21 adults, 8 women and 13 men, between the ages of 20 and 55
> • from Afghanistan, Iraq, Somalia, Lebanon, Sri Lanka, Thailand, Rumania and Turkey.

foreign language in China we need another example; I think examples are more telling and more important. This is an example from Denmark, and this is teaching Danish as a foreign or second language, the language of the country like Chinese in China.

In this case the learners are adults who are in fact immigrants or asylum seekers in Denmark. This kind of learner may not be the ones taught in Chinese classes, but the point is they are learning the language of the country in the country, like learning Chinese in China. They were a group of 21 adults, 8 women and 13 men of different ages. They were from many countries as maybe your learners are, from Afghanistan, Iraq, Somalia, Lebanon, Sri Lanka, Thailand, Romania and Turkey. In other words, countries from where they were coming to seek migration or asylum.

In the classroom, the learners were already curious. Sometimes we have to stimulate curiosity, but in this case, they were wondering about what happened to the older generation in Denmark. How do Danish people treat their older people? They did not understand, because it seemed from their observation of the society around them, that Danish people are not interested in their parents and the older generation. This was a contrast with their own societies, Afghanistan, Iraq, Sri Lanka and so on. They were curious about what happens in Danish society to the older people.

The teachers prepared lessons using objectives. By the end of the lessons, what they wanted was that their learners would know how to interpret and compare the life of

> **Origin of project**
> - classroom discussion about our relation to our parents and to the elderly in general
>
> - incomprehension about the apparent lack of interest the Danes have for their elderly relatives – especially parents → curiosity

人的生活；学会如何将其本国老年人的生活与丹麦老年人的生活进行比较。他们还应该学会如何更加深入地研究。老师不会告诉他们所有的知识，毕竟老师自己也不一定什么都知道，所以学生必须要自己来探索丹麦老年人的状况。为此，他们不得不用到丹麦语，也就是他们的外语，来进行探究。他们必须要学会提问，这些问题不是只用作口语练习的问题，而是真正的交际。到课程结束时，他们还要了解丹麦以及他们本国的现状，并对母国以及丹麦人的信仰和行为进行批判性分析。

> * *Objectives*: By the end, learners will
>
> * know how to interpret and compare life as a senior citizen in the learners' homelands;
>
> * Know how to find out about old people in Denmark and practice language with real questions;
>
> * Know how to critically analyse own and other beliefs about old people;
>
> * Know that... about the situation for old people in Denmark.

　　他们如何进行自主学习呢？他们设计了一个问卷。首先他们会谈自己祖国的情况，所有来自阿富汗的人组成了一个小组，所有来自斯里兰卡的人组成一个小组等等。他们用本国语言进行交流，讨论"我们"在"我们的"社会对老年人是怎样的态度。之后老师会提出一些问题。我们这里的问题都是用英语列出来的，当然这些问题最初都用丹麦语提出的。

　　这些就是老师给出的问题，这些问题可以让学生思考他们自己国家的情况，并就此展开课堂讨论。他们根据自己国家的实际情况来回答这些问题，然后将信息汇总到计算机、地图等工具上并进行讨论。这就意味着他们其实是在用丹麦语来讨论对他们而言十分重要的话题，这本身就很有启发性，也很重要。他们把所有有关自己国家的信息都保存在电脑上，以便与他们在课堂上讨论的内容进行比照，这也可以用于和丹麦的情况进行比较。

　　然后老师会教给学生部分"是什么的知识"，学生会知道丹麦的现状。老师还会给他们提供一些数据，让他们读一些文章或看电视节目。譬如，老师复印了一些以老年人为主题的欧洲名画，并将之作为讨论的主题。这些绘

senior citizens or old persons in their own country; know how to compare that with the life of older people in Denmark. They will also know how to find out more. The teachers will not tell them everything, and the teachers do not know everything about what happens in Denmark. So the learners will have to learn how to discover for themselves about older people in Denmark, and to do so they have to use Danish, their foreign language, to discover things. They have to be able to ask questions, and these are not practice questions but real questions. They also need, by the end of this lesson, to know what happens in Denmark, but also in their own country, and then critically analyse their own beliefs and practices from their own countries, and those of people in Denmark.

How did they learn for themselves? They invented a questionnaire. But first of all they talked about their own country. All the people from Afghanistan were in a group, all the people from Sri Lanka were in a group and so on. They talked in their own language about what 'we' do in 'our' own society with old people. The teachers gave them some questions. These questions here are in English, but of course originally they were in Danish.

Those are the questions that the teachers gave them to make them think about their own country and that become part of the classroom discussion. They answered the questions for their own country and each group put the information on a computer and on a map and talked about it. This meant that they were talking in Danish

---

Finding out - Questionnaire

- **Step 1:** Classes divided into national groups, use their mother tongue in their discussions while their results and presentations in Danish.

- **Senior citizens in your homeland**

  - Who is considered to be a senior citizen?
  - When do you become a senior citizen?
  - Does being a senior citizen have high or low status/prestige?
  - How/where does a senior citizen live?
  - How does a senior citizen support himself/herself?
  - How does a senior citizen pass the time?
  - Who helps/supports senior citizens?
  - What happens if a senior citizen becomes ill?
  - What happens when a senior citizen dies?

  Answers typed on computers and pinned on a map of the world next to the appropriate country.

---

about something which was very important to them, and that's intellectually stimulating and important. They put all the information they had about their own country on a computer in order to compare with what they know about their own countries represented in the classroom, so that they can compare and contrast when they have information about Denmark.

The teacher then gave them some but not all 'knowledge that', knowledge about Denmark, what happens in Denmark, gave them statistics, articles to read, and showed them programmes from television. For example, the teachers copied some famous paintings by European painters of old people and that became a topic

画可以展示出欧洲文化是如何表现老人形象的。

Step 2 Same questionnaire used for learners' expectations of Denmark - results noted on OHP for later comparison and evaluation

Step 3 Teachers show videos, pictures, short texts, newspaper articles and TV-programmes showing different facets of life as a senior citizen, to broaden the learners' knowledge that.

- Example: Copies of paintings by famous European painters showing old people → critically analyse how European artists have portrayed the elderly through the ages

  下一步就是进行实地考察，这就是在母语国学语言和在非母语国学语言的差别。比如在中国学汉语，学生就可以去实地考察：他们可以到外面收集数据，自己去挖掘和探索。因为这些学生的语言能力还不是特别高，所以为了做好课外实际交流的准备，他们会事先练习一下准备好的问题。此外他们还要把对话进行录音和录像。在拜访当地的一个老年之家之前，他们会先进行课堂练习。然后，他们分成三个小组，分别前往老年人聚居且比较活跃的地方。其中一组去了当地的一所医院，并和负责护理老年人的护士进行了沟通。另一个小组去了当地的一所老年大学，和这里的老师、学生聊天。还有一个小组走进了公社；公社这个概念源于 20 世纪 60 年代，人们不是单独居住，而是聚居在一起。这个公社里的人都已经有 50 多岁了，他们的孩子都不在身边，所以他们就一起住进了公社。学生们也和这些人进行了交流。当然，去什么地方考察主要取决于老师可以安排到什么样的地方，能联系到什么样的人。

  考察结束之后，学生就会把他们收集到的信息拿到课堂上与其他小组的同学分享。每一组还要在互联网上以及当地图书馆里收集更多的信息，这样的话他们就有机会锻炼自己的阅读能力，发现更多和主题相关的信息。重点是，每一小组的活动内容都有所不同，这样就可以吸引和激励其他小组的成员去聆听他们的展示，从而了解其他组都做了哪些工作。换句话说，每一个小组都要向其他小组展示自己所获得的信息，然后讨论和交流他们所挖掘到的这些信息。他们现在要分析这些从社会生活中收集来的数据。

for discussion as well. The painting can show you how older people are represented in the culture of Europe.

The next step is to do field work. This is the difference between learning the language in the country where it is spoken and learning the language in another country. If they are learning Chinese in China, learners can do field work: they can go out and collect data and find out things for themselves. Because these are learners who were not very proficient yet, in the classroom they prepared to go out and use Danish with real people outside the classroom by practicing the questions they planned to use. They had recorders to record conversations and they had video cameras. They practiced using them in the classroom before they went as a whole group to visit a local residence for older people. Then in three separate groups, they went to three different places where older people live and are active. One group went to a local hospital, and talked to somebody who is responsible for older people. Secondly, another group went to a university for older people, and talked to the students and the teachers. The third group went to visit a commune; the commune idea came from the 1960s where people lived together not in separate houses but lived together as a group. Here was a group of people who were over 50. Their children had left home so they lived together in a commune. And the students talked to those people too. The choice of places to visit was a matter of what the teacher could arrange and the contacts the teacher had.

Step 4 : fieldwork

Data collection – finding out

In classroom: Questions prepared and practice with recorders and cameras

Whole group visited residence for old people

First sub-group visited local hospital and talked to lady responsible for aids for disabled.

Second sub-group visited a nearby folk high school for seniors - interviewed teacher and people on course

Third sub-group visited a commune for people over 50 without children living at home

• Extra information gathered by each group (local library, Internet, etc.)

Each group collected information and then of course they came back to the classroom and shared the information with the other groups in the class. Each group also collected further information from the library, the Internet and so on. So that gave them an opportunity to use their reading skills to find out more information about the topic. The important point is that each group had done something different, so it was interesting and motivating for the other groups to listen to the presentations and to know about what each group had done. In other words, they presented their information to the other groups and had discussions

```
Step 5 : reporting and analysing [knowing how]

• Groups make wall-charts with pictures taken and
  explanatory texts
• Present results to other groups – questions and
  answers

Two guests speakers: (knowing that)
- senior citizen – no longer working but still active
- person from local town hall - talked about rights,
  privileges and duties as a senior citizen.
```

最后老师会请两位客座发言人，他们会进一步补充"是什么的知识"。其中一位本身就是老人，他会讲一讲自己的生活。另一位是地方官员，来自地方市政厅，他会谈一谈老年人的权利、特权和责任。

所以这个过程就融合了两个方面，一是学生知道了如何自主地获取信息，二是学生收获了老师和客座嘉宾所提供的知识。我希望大家在中国教汉语可以参考这样的例子。

评价与评估

下面我们要来讲一下评价和评估。我们讲过课程规划中重要的是要设计教学目标，这样在课程结束的时候，学生能够知道"是什么的知识"和"怎么做的知识"。这就是一个评价的起点。但是这个过程并不简单。

评估 vs. 评价

首先，我想区别一下"评价"和"评估"这两个概念。英语里这两个词是有差别的，但不是所有语言都可以将之区别开，比如在其他欧洲语言里，这两个词就没有差别。因此想要区分这两个词并不容易，但更重要的是这两个词的含义。评估是针对老师教学的，而评价是学生去判断自己是否达到了老师为他们设立的学习目标。首先，老师要自问关于教而不是学的问题。我们要问自己，"在课堂上我是否完成了在办公室或在家里制订的备课计划？"我们还要问自己，"我教得好不好？"假如我的确是按照计划教学的，那么教学效果如何？效果好吗？"好"只用于我对某一事情表示"赞许"，如果

and questions and answers about what they discovered. They were now analysing data which they had collected themselves from the society around them.

Finally the teachers invited two guest speakers, who could add to the 'knowledge that' which the students had acquired for themselves. They could provide more 'knowledge that'. One was a man who came and talked about his life as a senior citizen. Another was someone of more official nature, from the local town hall, who talked about the rights and privileges and duties as a senior citizen.

This was then a combination of knowing how to get information for yourself and knowledge that which the teacher gives or which the invited speakers give. I hope the example gives some ideas for teaching Chinese in China.

Assessment and Evaluation

So the next step is to think about assessment and evaluation. The important thing is to remember that we teachers have planned our lessons in terms of the objectives, so we know that we hope that by the end of the lesson, our learners will know that and our learners will know how. So that gives us a starting point for deciding how to assess. But it's not easy.

Evaluation contrasted with assessment

First of all, I want to make a distinction between assessment and evaluation. This is a distinction which is possible in English, but not in all languages, and not in other European languages for example. It is therefore sometimes difficult to clarify the difference but the important thing is what these words mean. Evaluation is a matter of questions for teachers about teaching, whereas assessment is a matter of questions for learners to find out if they have learnt what we hope they have learnt. First of all, teachers need to ask themselves questions about teaching before we ask questions about learning. Teachers need to ask themselves, 'Is what I am doing in the classroom what I want to do, what I plan to do when I was sitting at my office or at home planning my lessons?' We also need to ask: 'Are my lessons good?' Let's assume that I am in fact teaching what I plan to teach. Is it working? Is it good? The word 'good' means nothing except 'I approve of' something. So 'good' is an empty word until we give it some content and we need to ask 'What do we mean by "good" in this case? Are my lessons clear and well-structured? Are the students learning what I want them to learn? Do my lessons motivate students? Do my lessons make them curious about the other culture?'

How do I know the answers to those questions? The best way is to have a

我们说不出具体好在哪里，这个词就显得空洞无味。所以我们要自问，"当我们说这很'好'时究竟意味着什么？我的课程结构足够清晰合理吗？学生们达到了预期学习目标了吗？我的课程能激励学生吗？学生们是否能因此对其他文化产生兴趣？"

我如何才能知道这些问题的答案？最好的方法是要有一个有判断力的朋友，或者就是另外一位老师，他来听你的课，在你旁边观察。他既然是你的朋友，在提意见的时候就会相对温和，不会太咄咄逼人。但是他必须具有批判性，这样才能帮助我们认真思考自己的教学过程。当然，你也可以成为这个老师的有判断力的朋友，你们两个可以相互旁听，相互提意见。

关于教学，以上都是需要我们自问的问题。如果教得不好，我们也不能指望学生学得好。所以我们最终要问自己的就是："我的课成功吗？教得好而且也很成功？"这时，我们就需要知道学生究竟学到了什么，也就需要提出评价的问题。这个问题就是："我的课成功吗？成功究竟指的是什么意思？"它是指大部分学生都能达到一个不错的水平吗？同样，如果我们不给"不错"这个词加入一些实质性的东西，它就会显得很空洞。所以我们要找到学习效果的根据，也就是从评价中找到根据，比如通过考试这种评价方式寻找根据，但考试并不是唯一的评价方式。我们还可以想出两种类型的评价，一种来自教师，另一种来自课堂以外，也就是类似于国家考试这种由学校以外的机构所组织的考试。

跨文化交际能力评价

这些都是耳熟能详的方法，但关键是我们要把这些方法运用到跨文化的语言教学中。换句话说，当涉及学习者的学习效果时，我们可以问哪些问题？在传统的语言教学里，我们通过考试问学生一些问题，考查他们是不是掌握了"是什么的知识"。第二类问题，在传统的语言教学中我们不会问到，但在涉及跨文化学习的商界却会出现。这类问题大致涉及学习者如何感知另一种文化并与之互动。比如，在商界这些问题可以具体化为：这个人是否能够到另外一个国家去工作并且成功地完成任务？在商界这是一个非常重要的问题，因为公司要斥巨资把经理或是其他人派到海外去工作，如果这个人在某种程度上不具备跨文化交际的能力，钱就白花了，这个人就会被召回。第三，

critical friend, another teacher who will come and observe what you are teaching, and as a friend be friendly, not aggressive, in their comments. Nonetheless, the friend should be critical to help us to think carefully about what we are doing. And of course one can be a critical friend for one's critical friend.

Evaluation – Questions for teachers [Assessment – Questions for learners]

• Am I doing in practice what I planned to do?
• Are my lessons 'good' =
   • are my lessons clear and well structured?
   • are the students learning what I want them to learn?
   • do my lessons motivate students?
• EVIDENCE: help from a 'critical friend' who observes and discusses

• Are my lessons 'successful' =   • Do (most of) my students reach a good level? • EVIDENCE: assessment (by teacher AND/OR external examination)

Those are some of the questions which we need to ask about our teaching. Because if our teaching is not good, then we can't expect our learners to learn. In other words, as a final question, we have to ask: 'Are my lessons successful? Good but also successful?' It is at this point that we need to know to what the learners have learnt. We need to ask questions about assessment. The question is: 'Are my lessons successful and what do we mean by successful?' Does it mean most students reach a good level? Again the word is empty until we fill it with something, by defining the level which we consider 'good'. Then we need the evidence for the learning, i.e. the evidence from assessment, from tests for example, but tests are not the only means of assessment. We can also think of two kinds of assessment, by the teacher and by someone who is outside the classroom. In other words, by examinations by some other external body, e.g. state examinations.

Assessment of intercultural competence

This is all familiar ground, but we need to apply it to intercultural language teaching. In other words, what questions can we address to learners about their learning? In traditional language teaching, we have examinations which ask questions to find out the 'knowledge that' that learners have acquired. A second type of question is a question which we don't traditionally ask in language teaching but which is asked in the business world with respect to intercultural learning. That is, how do learners feel or react to other cultures. For example, in the business world, the question often asked is: 'Will this person be able to go and work in another country and be successful?' That's a very important question in the world of business because they might spend a lot of money sending managers and so

采用更为现代的教学语言以及教育方法，我们可以问，学习者"能做"什么。也就是说，他们拥有哪些"怎么做的知识"。在教育界，我们可以思考，是否有一些测试、任务或某种活动不仅能帮助我们检测"是什么的知识"，还可以检测"怎么做的知识"？所以"能做"（can do）这个词是非常重要的。

```
ASSESSMENT – Questions for learners
            WHAT TO ASSESS?

1. What learners know      →    traditional education exams

2. How learners feel/react →    business – able to work abroad?

3. What learners can do    →    new education tests or tasks
```

现在我们来详细地探讨一下这些问题。我们可以先来看一下商业领域的评价手段。弥尔顿·贝内特（Milton Bennett, 1993）在商界可谓赫赫有名，因为他创造了一套测试方法，可以检测出处在异国文化中的人是如何感受、如何做出反应的。这种反应分为不同的阶段，最开始可能是"拒绝"，处在这种状态下的人不愿与异国文化产生任何接触。还有一些人会进入到第二阶段，就是"防御"，人们觉得必须要保护自己的文化和生活方式，以免受周围文化的侵扰。第三个阶段是"弱化"，人们的反应是"好的，我来到中国了，我知道这种文化确实和我所处的文化不一样。但是在表象之下我们都是一样的，都是人类"。他把这几个阶段都称为"民族中心主义"。也就是说，以我自己为例，我仍处于英语的思维方式之中。在第一阶段，我还是愿意保留英国人的生活方式和思维习惯，尽管我身处中国，我却不想和中国的文化发生任何关系。在第二阶段，我会想，"嗯，中国不错，但是英国更好"，我会捍卫自己的文化。在第三阶段，我会说，"啊，中国不错，英国也不错，实际上这都是表象，表象之下我们其实都是一样的。"但是在这三个阶段中我始终是从英国人的角度思考的。

第四个阶段是贝内特所说的"接受"，在这个阶段我开始接受中国的文化、中国人的做事方式，因为"文化是一个动词"。我接受中国的文化，并且意

on to work in other countries. If that person is in some way not inter-culturally competent, then the money is wasted and they have to come home. Thirdly, we can ask questions in a more modern way of teaching languages and education generally, i.e. questions about what learners 'can do'. In other words, what 'knowledge how' do they have? In the education world, we can now begin to think about tests or tasks or some kind of activity where we can find out not only knowledge that but knowledge how. The phrase 'can do' becomes very important.

Let me take these issues in more detail and take the second approach first, the one from the business world. In the business world, Milton Bennett (1993) is very famous because he has produced a means of testing how people feel and how they react when they are in another culture. There are different levels of reaction. Moving from left to right on the screen, there are reactions which are 'denial'. This describes people who don't want to have any contact with other cultures. There are those who move to a stage that he calls 'defence', that is that people feel that they need to defend their own culture and way of life against the new one that they are experiencing. Then there is the third stage where people 'minimise', that is their reaction is to say 'Oh well yes I am in China, I know it's different but beneath the skin we are all the same, we are all human beings.' All of those stages he calls 'ethnocentric'. In other words, in my case this would mean that I still remain within my English way of thinking. In the first stage, I would say I want to remain English. I don't want anything to do with China even though I am here. In the second stage, I would think 'Oh, yes, China is nice but England is better'. I defend my own culture. In the third stage I would say, 'Ah, China is nice, England is nice and actually beneath the skin we are all the same.' But in all of these three stages I am still thinking from my English point of view.

The next stage is what Bennett calls 'acceptance' where I would begin to accept Chinese culture, in other words, a Chinese way of doing things since 'Culture is a verb'. I accept and see that China has its own values, beliefs and ways of doing things.

The next stage is to begin to adapt to that Chinese way of

---

2. HOW LEARNERS FEEL/REACT
Developmental Model of Intercultural Sensitivity - Bennett

- Denial →Defence → Minimization →Acceptance → Adaptation → Integration

Denial →Defence → Minimization = ETHNOCENTRISM
Acceptance → Adaptation → Integration = ETHNORELATIVISM

- 'a continuum of increasing sophistication in dealing with cultural differences'
- 'refers to the ability to discriminate and experience relevant cultural differences'

http://www.idrinstitute.org/allegati/IDRI_t_Pubblicazioni/47/FILE_Documento_Bennett_DMIS_12pp_quotes_rev_2011.pdf

识到中国拥有其独特的价值观、信仰体系和行为方式。

第五个阶段是要适应中国的行为方式，我会开始以中国人的方式来行为处事。或许我会开始以中国人的方式来思考，去探索一些更深刻的层面，接纳更深层次的中国人的思维方式和存在方式。最后我会融入，我想成为一个中国人。这是整个反应链上的最后一站，很大程度上也受制于中国人是否愿意接纳我成为他们中的一员。但是一般人很难达到这个阶段，如果人们能进入"接受"的阶段，并能部分到达"接纳"的阶段，那么他们就可以成功地在商界发展了。

实际上有很多方法可以用来测试这些反应，从而判断出一个人正处于哪个反应阶段。在商界有一个基于贝内特理论的非常有名的测试方法叫做"跨文化发展能力鉴定"，也称作"纸笔测试"，即在纸上或网上回答问题。系统会根据你的回答生成分析报告，老板或外派人员本人就知道他是否能够胜任海外工作。这个是以商界为例的具体案例，许多类似的网站可以提供这种评价，如"跨文化发展能力鉴定"（Intercultural Development Inventory）、"跨文化冲突模式鉴定"（Intercultural Conflicts Style Inventory）、"跨文化反应能力鉴定"（Intercultural Readiness Check）等等。

---

2. HOW LEARNERS FEEL/REACT
(Business)

EXAMPLE
- Intercultural Development Inventory – based on Bennett
- 50 questions – taken either in paper and pencil form or online.
- produces 'profile' of intercultural competence

- Testers attend an intensive, IDI Qualifying Seminar (IDI QS) - 3 days

- http://idiinventory.com/

这就是商界的情况了。对于教育界来说，我觉得可能还需要问一些其他的问题，比如，"学习者在课后都**学到**了什么知识？他们又将如何**运用**这些知识？"

doing things, and I would begin to do things in the Chinese way. Maybe I begin to think in a Chinese way, to adapt some of the deeper aspects, some of the deeper rules of a Chinese way of thinking and being. And finally, maybe I integrate. I want to become a Chinese. That's the furthest point on the continuum which also depends on Chinese people accepting me as Chinese. That's not always the case. It's unusual for people to move all the way to the right side, but it is hoped that they will move to 'acceptance' and some kind of 'adaptation', so

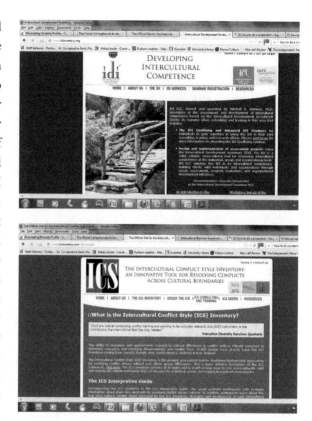

that in the business world they can be successful.

There are many ways of testing those reactions and deciding which stage someone has reached. One test which is very well known in the business world is the 'intercultural development inventory', which is based on the Bennett's theory. It's a 'paper and pencil test', i.e. answering a number of questions on paper or online and from these answers the inventory produces a profile, which gives the employer or the person who might be sent for example to China to work, a profile of how likely it is that the person who has taken the test will be successful in a foreign assignment. This is an example which is very specific to the business world, and there are lots of websites offering this kind of assessment: the Intercultural Development Inventory, Intercultural Conflicts Style Inventory, the Intercultural Readiness Check and so on.

That is the business world. In the education world, I think there are other questions which we need to ask, questions such as: 'What do learners *know* after we have taught them, and what they can *do* after what we have taught them?'

教育评价

我们来看看回答这两个问题的不同方式。首先我想再提醒大家一下几种不同的评价方式，然后我们再来具体地谈谈对跨文化能力的评价。

一种评价方式叫做"**总结性评价**"。在一节课或是一系列课程结束之后，教师用这种方法来评价学生的学习效果。此外还有"**形成性评价**"，就是在上课的过程中，随时了解学生学到了什么，以决定是不是需要调整课程，改进效果，因为有的时候学生并不像预期中学得那么好。至于方法，如果你想了解学生学到了哪些"是什么的知识"，你可以给他们做测试。在"传统的"语言教学中，我们会通过语言测试来检测学生是不是掌握了语法知识。如果学生正确地回答出一些挑选好的问题，我们可以假设他们已经掌握了其他相关的知识点。当涉及"怎么做的知识"时，我们可以检测学生能"**做**"什么，这样我们就能判断出他们是否学会了应用知识。该如何操作呢？我们要观察学生的口语和写作，或者给他们一些任务看他们能否完成。我们可以分析他们的做题过程，比如可以让他们进行角色扮演，看他们能否完成角色扮演的目标，在这个过程中特别要检测的是学生能否得体地、有礼貌地使用语言来达到交际的目的。我们也可以用一种反思性的方式来看他们是不是学会了应用知识，比如要求他们在任务完成之后写一个反思，然后分析该反思。这样做的目的是通过他们**已完成的任务**来检测他们学会了多少"**怎么做的知识**"。其实这些方法都是比较司空见惯的。

```
1. WHAT LEARNERS KNOW
3. WHAT LEARNERS CAN DO
(education)

• Purpose 1: to find out how well learners have learnt = summative
• Purpose 2: to find out how well learners are learning = formative

Methods:
• finding out what learners know = knowledge that
    • tests of what they say (= [some] knowledge that)

• finding out what learners can do = knowledge how
    • observations of learners doing
    • analysis of documents of products (i.e. what has been done)
```

那么由谁来评价？为什么这样评价？首先，老师是评价者，他要了解学生是不是学到了知识，从而规划下一阶段的教学。当然，在中学或大学中，我们

Assessment in education

Let's look at different ways of answering those two questions. Let me first remind you about different kinds of assessment and then I will talk more specifically about intercultural competence assessment.

As we know, one kind of assessment is *summative*. At the end of one or more lessons or a course, the teacher assesses what the learners have learnt. And there is *formative* assessment, where during the course, the teacher tries to find out what the learners are learning, and whether they need to change the course to make it more effective, maybe because learners are not learning as well as the teacher would like. In terms of methods, when we want to find out what 'knowledge that' learners have, we give them tests. And in 'traditional' language teaching, we give learners tests to find out what 'knowledge that' they have about the grammar of a language. If they are successfully answering a selection of questions, then we hope that is an indication that they know other things just as well. When we come to 'knowledge how', we try to find out what learners can *do*, and that will give us some idea of their knowledge how. How do we do that? We observe learners speaking or writing, or we give them a task to do and see how successfully they can accomplish it. We analyse what they are doing as they are doing it. We can for example put them in a role play and find out if they can do what is required in the role play, particularly to find out if they can use language appropriately and politely, communicatively. We can also find out what they can do retrospectively, for example by asking them to write some kind of response to a task, and then analyse what they have written after it is completed. In that sense we can find out what they *can do* from what they *have done*. This is all familiar, I am sure.

Now what about who assesses and why? Teachers assess to know if learners have learnt and to plan the next step of teaching. And of course in schools and universities, we have to tell parents or learners themselves, if they are being successful. But learners too can assess. That's perhaps less traditional, but learners can assess themselves and find out for themselves if they are being successful. Then thirdly, we have examination authorities, which will give a certificate.

Who assesses and why?

- 1. Teacher – to know if learners have learned, to plan next stage of teaching [and to report to parents, learners themselves, etc.]
- 2. Learners – to know if they have learned AND to plan next stage of learning
- 3. Examination authorities – to give a certificate [and report to society] = much 'at stake' = 'high stakes testing']
  - NOT YET POSSIBLE FOR INTERCULTURAL COMPETENCE

必须要告诉家长和学生本人他们的学习是否成功。但学生自己也可以进行评价。这种做法可能并不常见，但是学生可以进行自我评价，并且能够判断自己在学习过程中成功与否。第三是权威的考试机构，他们能够颁发相关的证书。这个证书不是向家长和学生汇报，而是要对社会做交代，证明这个人学得很成功。这就是所谓的"高风险"评价。这个评价非常重要，因为它可以决定一个人的前途，决定他是否能够成功，是否能找到工作，是否能被大学录取。

这些就是我们能够为语言能力所做的了，大家应该都很熟悉，但是关键在于我们能为跨文化交际能力做多少。恐怕第三点到现在还无法实现，现在还没有可行的"高风险"的跨文化考试。这个有点让人失望，因为我们知道这种"高风险"的跨文化交际证书对于学生来讲至关重要，也会激励他们进一步学习。但是，我们必须要开诚布公地讲，现在这种可靠的、有效的、有制度保障的"高风险"跨文化交际考试还不存在。倒是有一些实验在做这方面的努力，但目前为止他们还不是特别令人满意，在这里我就不展开描述了。

这就意味着我们现在只有一、二两种评价方式：教师评价和学生评价。由教师去评价学生的能力，就意味着作为老师，我们需要让学生演示他们所掌握的某些知识，从而判断出学生学到了什么或者能做什么。"展示"意味着老师能够观察学生能做什么。教师还要看学生是否做得"好"，但我刚才也说了，"好"是很空洞的词，它只表示你赞同某事。《牛津英语词典》是这样对"好"进行定义的，我想汉语词典里面应该也有类似的表达。

Assessment – deciding what is 'good' competence

- The definition of 'good' in the *Oxford English Dictionary*.
  - As a general adjective of commendation, implying that the thing described is of high or satisfactory quality [standard], suitable for some purpose, or worthy of approval.
- But WHY?
- When/why do you say learners' **language** competence is good? … Your criteria/standards?
- NATIVE SPEAKER?

"好"是一个表示赞许的形容词，意味着其所描述的事物质量或水平令人满意，能够满足某些目的，因而值得赞扬。所以如果我在你的作业上写了"好"，这至多能表明"我赞赏你的作业"，但是这并没有说出我**为什么赞赏**

The certificate is not a report to the parents or the students, but a report to society that a learner has been successful. This is the so-called 'high-stakes' kind of assessment. It's very important because it makes a difference in the career of a learner and their being successful, getting a job or not, and being admitted to university or not.

All of that is familiar and what we do for language competence. The question is how much we can do for intercultural competence. And I think I have to disappoint you in Number Three, because at this moment, it's not possible to my knowledge to produce 'high-stakes' examinations for intercultural competence. That is a disappointment, because we know that 'high-stakes' certificates of intercultural competence would be important to the learners, and would also motivate them in their learning. But we have to be honest that at the moment, 'high-stakes' examinations which are reliable and valid and which an examinations system can be sure of, do not exist. There are experiments, but I am not going to describe experiments to you because they are not yet satisfactory.

So that means that we are left with Number One and Number Two: teacher assessment and learner assessment. Teacher assessment of learners' competence means we need as teachers to ask our students to demonstrate some aspects of what they know, which will give us some insight into their 'knowledge that' or what they can do, their 'knowledge how'. 'Demonstrating' means that the teacher can observe what the learner can do. The teacher also needs to see whether what the learner can do is 'good', but as I said earlier 'good' is an empty word. 'Good' means nothing except approval. Here is a definition from *The Oxford English Dictionary*. I assume one would find something similar in a Chinese dictionary.

The word 'good' is an adjective of commendation, implying that the thing described is of high or satisfactory quality or standard, and that is suitable for some purposes or worthy of approval. So if I write 'good' on a learner's homework, all that means is 'I approve'. It doesn't tell the learner anything about *why* I approve. The learner needs to know therefore what the criteria are for saying that something is good.

---

1. Teacher assessment
Criterion-referenced assessment

- measures an individual's performance based on a predefined standard, rather than relative to the performance of others

- QUESTION: Which criteria/standards for what learners know about language [knowledge that]?
- TRADITIONAL ANSWER : Grammar book and dictionary of 'native speaker'

- QUESTION: Which criteria for what learners can do [knowledge how]?
- TRADITIONAL ANSWER: ... like a native speaker

你的作业。学生需要了解"好"的标准是什么。我们是不是要以母语者的标准去评价"这是好的"？在评价语言能力时，我们常常是这样做的。我们会说，这基本上讲得很地道了，或者从某种程度上说，很像母语者了。但这种方法在今天其实是充满争议，饱受诟病的。

但是我们可以暂且搁置这个争论，因为在讨论跨文化交际能力时使用母语者作为衡量标准是不合适的。在跨文化交际能力中我们需要其他的衡量标准。我们需要观察学习者，看他们作为**跨文化语言者**能做些什么、说些什么。像以前一样，我们要确定在教学结束之后学生应该学会什么，但这个"是什么的知识"和母语者所学到的不完全一致。其次，跨文化交际能力中所教授的"怎么做的知识"也与母语者所学有所差异。

通过"礼貌"这个概念建立起了一层联系。"礼貌"既是交际能力中的一个元素，又与跨文化交际能力休戚相关。

---

1. Teacher assessment
EXAMPLE:
Assessing 'appropriate/ polite' use of language

- **Knowledge that:**
  - give rules for different kinds of letter writing, e.g. [in English] address in top right of page, etc.

- **Knowledge how:**
  - write a letter to your boss asking for an extra holiday
  - Role-play in real time: write an email exchange with your boss to ask for an extra holiday [teacher acts as boss]

- **DEFINE LEVELS:** *Common European Framework of Reference for Languages* (section 5.2.2.5)
- **Available in Chinese**

比如，学习者需要知道如何写正式或是非正式的信件，或者是在正式或非正式的场合里用口语与他人交流。正式场合的例子就是向老板请假。这既可以是一次对写作的评价，也可以是一次对利用口语进行角色扮演的评价。下一步就要定义什么是"好"的回答，关于这一点，欧洲理事会 2001 年制定的《欧洲语言共同参考框架：学习、教学、评估》(CEFR) 已经做了大量的工作，这一框架也已经翻成汉语。[①] 对语言的适当或礼貌使用可分为许多

---

① 《欧洲语言共同参考框架：学习、教学、评估》汉语版已由外语教学与研究出版社于 2008 年出版。

Are we going to use the native speaker as a means of saying 'This is good'? When referring to language competence, often we do. We say this is 'almost like a native speaker', or some degree of being like a native speaker. That is an approach which is today much debated and criticised.

However, we can leave that debate aside because whether we use the native speaker for assessing language competence or not, for intercultural competence I would say it is not appropriate to use the native speaker. We need, for intercultural competence, other criteria. We need to be able to observe our learners and what they can do and say as *intercultural speakers*. As before we need to decide what our learners should know at the end of our teaching, what 'knowledge that' but it will be different from that of a native speaker. Secondly the 'knowledge how' for intercultural competence is also quite different from a native speaker.

There is a connection through the notion of politeness. This is the element of communicative competence which is connected with intercultural competence.

For example, learners have to know how to write a letter, a formal letter or an informal letter, or they have to interact orally in formal and informal situations. An example of a formal situation would be asking the boss for a holiday. This can be an assessment in written or in oral form with a role play for the latter. The next step is to define what is a 'good' response and here there is already much work done in the *Common European Framework of Reference for Languages: Learning, Teaching, Assessment* (CEFR) (Council of Europe, 2001) which also exists in Chinese translation. Here are the different level descriptions for appropriate or polite use of language:

Common European Framework of Reference for Languages: learning, teaching, assessment

	SOCIOLINGUISTIC APPROPRIATENESS
C2	Has a good command of idiomatic expressions and colloquialisms with awareness of connotative levels of meaning. Appreciates fully the sociolinguistic and sociocultural implications of language used by native speakers and can react accordingly. Can mediate effectively between speakers of the target language and that of his/her community of origin taking account of sociocultural and sociolinguistic differences.
C1	Can recognise a wide range of idiomatic expressions and colloquialisms, appreciating register shifts; may, however, need to confirm occasional details, especially if the accent is unfamiliar. Can follow films employing a considerable degree of slang and idiomatic usage. Can use language flexibly and effectively for social purposes, including emotional, allusive and joking usage.
B2	Can express him or herself confidently, clearly and politely in a formal or informal register, appropriate to the situation and person(s) concerned. Can with some effort keep up with and contribute to group discussions even when speech is fast and colloquial. Can sustain relationships with native speakers without unintentionally amusing or irritating them or requiring them to behave other than they would with a native speaker. Can express him or herself appropriately in situations and avoid crass errors of formulation.

不同的级别，且各有各的具体描述。

B1	*Can perform and respond to a wide range of language functions, using their most common exponents in a neutral register.* *Is aware of the salient politeness conventions and acts appropriately.* *Is aware of, and looks out for signs of, the most significant differences between the customs, usages, attitudes, values and beliefs prevalent in the community concerned and those of his or her own.*
A2	*Can perform and respond to basic language functions, such as information exchange and requests and express opinions and attitudes in a simple way.* *Can socialise simply but effectively using the simplest common expressions and following basic routines.*
	Can handle very short social exchanges, using everyday polite forms of greeting and address. Can make and respond to invitations, suggestions, apologies, etc.
A1	*Can establish basic social contact by using the simplest everyday polite forms of: greetings and farewells; introductions; saying please, thank you, sorry, etc.*

在这些标准里围绕某人"能做"什么展开，尽管采用了"能表现"、"能处理"这样的词汇，但它总是围绕"能"（can）这个词展开，因为这些标准用于描述"怎么做的知识"。

基于标准的跨文化交际能力评价

现在的问题是我们如何以类似的方式来描述跨文化交际能力。这其实就更难了。我们需要分析学习者具备多少跨文化交际中"是什么的知识"和"怎么做的知识"。对于跨文化来说，我们不仅要评价所获得的知识，比如，在丹麦老年人过得怎么样，这其实是很重要的，但我们还需要了解学生是不是能够自己发现、比较、对比照顾老年人的不同方法，并对此进行批判性地评估。

让我们进一步来看这个问题。在跨文化交际能力里，一共有四种知识，其中三种是"怎么做的知识"，一种是"是什么的知识"。我们需要知道我们的学生在这四个领域里都掌握了哪些知识。然后要建立一个纵向维度进行评价，像之前评价社会语言学能力中语言使用的礼貌和恰当程度那样。之后我们就要问这么一个问题：到底应该把学生的水平分成多少级，每一级的标准是什么？

这些问题依然悬而未决。我们知道应该把焦点放在哪里。不管学生来自越南、美国还是其他什么国家，他们都要比较中国和自己国家的事物。我们要判断学生是否有自主探索的能力，在现实生活中又是如何与人互动的。我

The criteria are formulated as what someone 'can do' although here the words used are 'can perform' or 'can handle'. It is always formulated as 'can' because these are descriptions of 'knowledge how'.

Assessing intercultural competence by criteria

The question now is how we can describe intercultural competence in a similar way. This is more difficult. We need to analyse what intercultural 'knowledge how' and 'knowledge that' learners have. We need to assess not only knowledge that/

From language competence to intercultural competence

- Assess what knowledge HOW and knowledge THAT learners have…
- [not 'cultural' [=ONLY knowledge that] but 'intercultural' = also knowledge how]

- Intercultural competence = 'know how to discover' + 'know how to compare' + 'know how to [critically] evaluate' + 'know that…'

about how senior citizens are treated in Denmark, to take that example, which is important, but we also need to find out, if they know how to or can discover for themselves and compare and contrast and critically evaluate, the different approaches to care for the elderly for example.

Let us look at this in more detail. In intercultural competence, there are four kinds of knowing: three kinds of knowing how and one kind of knowing that. We need to find out what our learners know in those four different areas. Then we need to create a vertical scale, like the one we saw above for sociolinguistic competence,

1. Teacher assessment
'horizontal' and 'vertical'

- Horizontal = for each component of IC
  - 'know how to discover'
  - 'know how to compare'
  - 'know how to evaluate critically'
  - 'know that'

- Vertical = levels/degrees of 'know how' and 'know that'
  - How many levels?
  - How to write criteria for each level?

for appropriateness and politeness. Then the question arises: How many levels should we have? What are the criteria for each level?

These are still unresolved questions. We know what we need to focus on. Our learners need to *compare* things in China and their own country, whether they are Vietnamese or Americans or whatever. We need to find out if they can *discover* for themselves. We need to find out how they can *interact in real time*. We need to find out if they can *evaluate critically* aspects of Chinese culture and their own in terms

们要判断他们是否可以**批判地评价**中国文化及自身文化中的某些侧面，比如**行为方式**、**信仰体系**和**价值观**。如果要教他们汉语的话，我们还需要了解他们已经掌握了哪些关于**中国的知识**。我们希望他们保持**好奇心**，从不同的角度来看待世界。

---

1. Teacher assessment
Assessment of intercultural competence
(= know that + know how)

- Know how to relate and compare some 'thing' in China with some 'thing' in our Vietnamese/American, etc. culture
- Know how to discover (knowledge about Chinese and about us Vietnamese/ Americans, etc.) AND how to interact in real time (with others)
- Know how to evaluate critically what Chinese do and what we Vietnamese /Americans, etc. do, believe in, values.
- Know that most Chinese most of the time do X, believe Y, value Z. AND
- Be curious, willing to decentre - i.e. attitudes

欧洲理事会做了一系列实验来解决以上这些问题。等这些实验有了明确的结果，大家可以去关注一下 (www.coe.int/lang)，这很重要。

跨文化交际能力的教师评价

与此同时，我认为我们应该关注教师评价，关注与我们的教学过程相适应的评价的重要性。如果我们想一想丹麦课程的例子就会发现，老师们是希望他们的学生能够自主**探索**、**比较**和**对比**。他们在课堂里已经完成了这些，所以为了评价学生在今后的学习中面对其他材料和话题是否还能做到自主探索、比较和对比，老师们需要布置一个类似的任务。比如老师可以说，"研究完老年人的问题，我们现在研究一下丹麦社会和文化是怎么对待年轻人和青少年的，然后把丹麦的情况和你们自己国家的情况，比如阿富汗、伊拉克的情况进行比较和对比。我会给你们一些材料、数据、文章和音频，比如对年轻人生活状况的访谈等，然后我希望大家分析一下这个话题，并将其与自己所了解的本国文化里年轻人的生活进行比较和对比"。换句话说，这种评价方式应该是和课堂教学相类似的。

然后我们再去评价学生的任务做得好不好。当然这其中涉及了大量的工

of what they *do*, what they *believe* in and their *values*. We also need to find out what *knowledge they have about* China if we are teaching them Chinese. We want them finally to be *curious* and see the world from a different angle.

> 1. Teacher assessment
> ### Criteria for Intercultural Competence?
>
> • Experiments but not yet useful to teachers...
>   • [INCA project – SEE APPENDIX, new CEFR project]
>
> • Alternative for teachers:
>   • Assess by similar tasks as in teaching
>   • Assess how much/well learners can do

There are experiments to address some of these questions taking place at the Council of Europe and it will be important to check the results when they arrive (*www.coe.int/lang*).

Teacher assessment of Intercultural Competence

In the meantime, I think we should focus on teacher assessment and the importance of assessing in accordance with the way we teach. If we think of the example of the course in Denmark, it is clear that the teachers want their learners to *discover* for themselves, and to *compare and contrast*. They have done that in the lessons, and in order to assess whether the students can do the same in the future with other material and topics, the teachers need a task which will be similar to what they have done with the students in the classroom. Instead of focusing upon old people, they might say 'For this assessment task I want you to focus upon how Danish society, Danish culture, deals with young people, teenagers, adolescents, and I want you to compare and contrast with your own society, Afghanistan, Iraq or wherever you come from. I'm going to give you some materials, some data and some texts to read and listen to, for example an interview with some young people about their life. And I want you to produce an analysis of the topic, and compare and contrast with what you know about young people in your own society.' In other words, the assessment has to be similar to the teaching.

Then we can assess

> EXAMPLE
> 'Old People'
>
> • Teacher provides documents about a similar event (Young people)
>   • In own society [USA or Vietnam]
>   • In China
>
> • Learners prepare an explanation for 'others' (explain to Chinese people what happens in USA/Vietnam OR to USA/Vietnamese what happens in China)

作。我的建议是如果你想改进自己的跨文化教学，与其他教师合作是很重要的。这不是一名教师可以做好的事情，因为整个过程很复杂，工作量很大。你必须要与他人一起努力。

再举一个例子，在教授有关圣诞贺卡的课程时，保加利亚的老师要如何评估自己的教学呢？关键是学生们要做一些准备，以便介绍本国的情况。所以如果美国学生在中国学汉语，那么布置给他们的作业就应该是用汉语向中国人讲述在美国赠送圣诞贺卡、生日贺卡或是其他贺卡的做法。这样做其实是在检测他们是如何周旋在两种文化之间、比较和对比他们所学得的知识。他们了解自己的社会，但他们如何用汉语向中国人传达和阐释这些情况呢？

跨文化交际能力的自我评价

学生也可以进行自我评价。实际上这种评价和分数无关，而是让学生更加关注自己的学习过程，更关注自己的能力，关注自己能把什么事情做好，又需要在哪些方面继续改善。在某些情况下，教师自身即是学生——当你在其他国家教汉语的时候，你会和来自其他文化的人打交道——这可能会帮助教师更加理解自己的学生所处的境地。

---

2. Learner assessment
Self-assessment

Purpose
NOT GIVE A GRADE BUT BECOME MORE CONSCIOUS OF OWN COMPETENCE

Teachers are also learners AND teachers who teach in another country have intercultural experience needing intercultural competence.

欧洲理事会 2010 年出版的《跨文化经历自传》可以看作是在跨文化交际能力中进行自我评价的一个例子。这个文献可以帮助学习者应对异国文化和思考自己的反应。这些都是以真人真事为蓝本的。比如，在中国学习汉语的美国或越南学生在评价自己在中国的生活经历时，就可以参考这本书。他们可以用其母语或汉语来进行这种反思，这主要取决于他们目前的语言能力，

how well the students can do the task. That of course means a lot of work. And my suggestion now is if you want to improve your intercultural teaching in practice, then it is important to work together with other teachers. It's not something an individual teacher can do for themselves, because it's too complicated and too much work. You have to share your efforts and work together.

To give another of the examples, how could the teacher from Bulgaria assess what she was doing in a lesson about Christmas cards? The important thing is that the learners will prepare an explanation of what happens in their own country. So if we are thinking of American students learning Chinese in China, then the task is to prepare something in Chinese to present to Chinese people about Christmas cards or birthday cards or something like that in their own society. This is then testing what they can do to mediate, to compare and contrast what they know. They know about things in their own society. But how they can explain and mediate to someone in Chinese society in Chinese?

Self-assessment of Intercultural Competence

Learners can also assess themselves. This is not a matter of giving grades, but of the learners becoming more aware of their own learning, and more conscious of their own competence, conscious about what they can do well or what they need to improve. In some circumstances teachers are learners – for example when Chinese people teach Chinese in another country and are interacting with people of another culture – and this may give them extra insight into their learners' experiences.

One example of self-assessment in intercultural competence is some recent work on the *Autobiography of Intercultural Encounters* created at the Council of Europe. This is a document which helps learners to react to and think about how they respond to strangeness. It can be through interaction with real people in real time. For example American or Vietnamese students learning Chinese in China can use this *Autobiography of Intercultural Encounters* (AIE) (Council of Europe, 2010) when they evaluate their experience of life in China. They can do it in Chinese or their own language depending on the level of their language competence, and

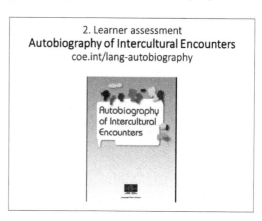

2. Learner assessment
Autobiography of Intercultural Encounters
coe.int/lang-autobiography

由此他们可以在课堂内外思考自己的跨文化学习。

　　《跨文化经历自传》中列出了很多问题，使用者要思考对他们而言很重要的一次跨文化经历，比如"我第一次去拜访一个中国家庭"。然后《跨文化经历自传》会基于跨文化交际及跨文化公民身份等理论提出一系列问题。这些问题会让他们从两个方面思考并写下跨文化的经历：比如学习者如何看待拜访中国家庭这个经历，同时还要思考中国家庭是如何看待他的。这是跨文化交际能力中的一个重要维度，即以他人的眼光来审视自己。《跨文化经历自传》就是要系统地培养学习者的这种能力，并思索下一步应该如何去应对，该作何改变，或为自己做些什么。也许他们的反应之一是"防御"："我觉得在中国的家庭中很难适应；我处在自己的文化中感到更惬意。"又或者是"适应"："我希望自己能更像中国人，融入中国的家庭。"

---

2. Learner assessment

The *Autobiography* – what is it?

- a series of questions and prompts
- structured to guide the user to reflect on an encounter with someone from another cultural group
- to describe and analyse from two perspectives – own and other
- to consider what they learnt from the encounter
- and what they will do as a consequence
- BASED ON THEORY OF INTERCULTURAL COMPETENCE

---

2. Learner assessment

The structure

1. NAMING THE ENCOUNTER	
2. DESCRIBING THE OTHER PERSON OR PEOPLE	
3. DESCRIBING YOUR FEELINGS	= 'feel/react'
4. ANALYSING THE OTHER PERSON'S FEELINGS	= 'can do'
5. ANALYSING SAME AND DIFFERENT	= 'can do'
6. ANALYSING TALKING TO EACH OTHER	= 'can do'
7. DISCOVERING / FINDING OUT MORE	= 'can do'
8. USING COMPARISONS TO UNDERSTAND	= 'can do'
9. THINKING BACK AND LOOKING FORWARD	= 'can do'

　　欧洲理事会的官方网站（http://www.coe.int/t/dg4/autobiography/default_EN.asp）上可以找到这些内容及其汉语版。

---

2. Learner assessment
Learning

8.   USING COMPARISONS TO UNDERSTAND
People often compare things in other groups or cultures with similar things in their own. Did you do this? Did it help you to understand what was happening?
For example:
The experience involved some things which were similar to what I know in my own group and these are the things I noticed...
There were some things which were different from my own group...

---

2. Learner assessment
Doing

9.   THINKING BACK AND LOOKING FORWARD
If, when you look back, you draw conclusions about the experience, what are they?
Complete as many of these as you can...
I **liked** the experience for the following reasons...
    (...)

Did the experience change you? How?

Did you decide to do something as a result of this experience? What did you do?

Will you decide to do something as a result of doing this Autobiography? If so what?

---

2. Learner assessment
Translated: Tony Hongtao Jing. Waseda University, Japan

跨文化经历自传
Autobiography of Intercultural Encounters

Michael Byram, Martyn Barrett, Julia Ipgrave,
Robert Jackson, María del Carmen Méndez García   著
荆红涛 译

---

they can begin to think about their intercultural learning inside but also outside the classroom.

The AIE is a series of questions. The user thinks of an encounter, something which was important to them: 'The first time I went and visited a Chinese family' for example. Then the AIE gives them a series of questions based on the theories of intercultural competence and intercultural citizenship. The questions ask them to think and write about their experience from two perspectives: How they felt about the experience of visiting a Chinese family for example, but also to try to think about how the Chinese family thought about them. This is an important dimension of intercultural competence. The ability to see ourselves as others see us. The AIE is an attempt to help learners to do this in a systematic way, and to think about what they will do as a consequence. How they will change and do something for themselves. Maybe their reaction was one of 'defence': 'I find it difficult to be in a Chinese family; I feel much happier in my own.' Or maybe their reaction is one of 'adaptation': 'I would like to act a bit more like Chinese people and a Chinese family.'

This is freely available on the Council of Europe website: *http://www.coe.int/t/*

还有另外一个版本，对那些在国外教授汉语的人来说也许有用。在国外，学习者可能没有机会在现实生活中与中国人接触，他们只能在虚拟现实里，比如媒体报道、报纸和网络中接触到中国人。在这第二个版本中，学习者可以选择曾经在报纸或网络中看到的某个特定的图像，甚至可以是他们曾欣赏过的一幅画，比如中国传统的绘画等，任何图像皆可，然后就这些图像进行提问，他们可以用汉语或自己的母语来回答。通过回答这些问题，他们可以分析出自己对现实或虚拟世界中的他者的反应。

结论

有关评价的若干问题，恐怕很难给出简单的答案，因为评价必须是基于教学的。如果教师备课时设定了教学目标，那么评价就应该基于这些目标来进行，要与老师上课内容相关。除此之外没有什么现成的解决方案。

我想要强调的是，对于教师而言，评价作为评估的一部分其实非常重要，这样他们才能知道自己的教学是否成功。评估对教师来讲也很重要，如果教师能拥有一个"有判断力的朋友"来帮助观察和分析他们的教学过程是否与教学目标相一致，他们就能知道自己的教学是否成功了。

其次，自我评价对学习者是很重要的，因为它可以帮助学习者意识到自己的学习状况，进而掌控自己的学习进程。但是对于那些在他国教学和学习的老师来说，自我评价也是很重要的，因为当这些老师迈出国门时，他们自己也变成了学生。他们必须做好学习的准备，并且意识到在异国他乡学习会遇到很多困难。所以我希望《跨文化经历自传》可以对同时作为教师和学生的各位有帮助，也对你们的学生有帮助。

dg4/autobiography/default_EN.asp, and there is a Chinese version being prepared. There is also another version which may be useful perhaps for those who teach Chinese in another country, where learners may not meet Chinese people in real life, but in virtual reality. They will meet China in the media, in the newspaper, on the Internet. The second version is one where the learner thinks about a particular image that they have met, that they found in the newspaper or on the Internet or whatever it may be. It could even be a painting that they have seen, a traditional Chinese painting for example. It can be any image. Then again there are a series of questions, and again they can answer in Chinese or their own language. By answering the questions, they analyse their own reaction to others, whether it's through image or in real life.

Conclusion

It is not possible to give simple answers to the question of assessment, because assessment has to come out to teaching. If teachers plan their teaching using objectives as I suggested earlier, then the assessment has to be based on the objectives and similar to what teachers have been teaching. There is then no ready-made solution.

What I have emphasised is that assessment is important to teachers as part of evaluation, so that they can know if their teaching is successful. Evaluation is important to teachers and if they have a 'critical friend' who helps them to observe and analyze whether they are doing what they want to do in a classroom, then they will know whether their teaching is successful.

Secondly, self-assessment is important to learners, because it helps them to be conscious of what they are doing and to be more in control of what they are learning. But self-assessment is also important to those teachers who are in another country and learning themselves, because when people go to another country as a teacher, they are also a learner. They have to expect to learn and to have difficulties as a learner in another country. I hope that these autobiographies will be useful to teachers as learners as well as to their own learners.

Conclusion

• Assessment is important to teachers = 'How I know if/what my learners are learning'

• Evaluation is important to teachers = 'How I know if I am teaching what I want to teach – and doing it well'

• Self-assessment is important to learners = 'How I become conscious of what I am learning'

• Self-assessment is important to teachers = 'How I become conscious of how I learn – and how my learners learn'

*　　　*　　　*

☺ 交流互动

提问人 1：我们是否可以说，跨文化能力旨在创造一个第三动态空间，在这个空间里，我们可以听到不同的声音，不同的文化能够共存？在评价方面，我们是否可以利用最近发展区理论？

Michael Byram：你说的第三空间是一个非常重要的概念，我自己没有用过这个术语。但当我谈及我们要作为一个媒介，把一个社会和一种文化阐释给另外一个社会和另外一种文化时，其实我就已经默认把这个人放在第三空间里了，这其实就是一个跨文化的空间。你可以把它称作第三空间，在这个空间里，你不需要掌握一个母语者的语言能力，重要的是要记住，不应该把学习者和处在任一社会或文化中的母语者进行比较。

这个问题还涉及了维果斯基著作中的最近发展区学习理论。理论里提到教师应该始终从学习者所处的位置出发，在学生已有的基础上增加新的知识点。这是对维果斯基理论的一种简化。但从某种意义上讲，这只是对好的教学方法的描述而已，它阐明教师应该知道自己学生的现状。就像在这几天的讲座里，我也要揣测各位的水平，我假设各位已经掌握了不少语言能力以及语言评价和交际能力方面的知识。正是基于这样的假设，我才会说"我想各位听说过语言评价。那现在让我们想一想如何利用你所知道的相关知识来进一步思考跨文化评价与教学问题"。

*　　　　*　　　　*

☺ Interaction and Communication

Questioner 1: Can we say that intercultural competence is also one of the purposes to create a certain space which is a dynamic space where multiple voices can be heard, or can co-exist? And about the assessment, can we also use the proxy development zone to test assessment?

Michael Byram: The notion of the third space is an important one. I haven't used that phrase myself. But when I began to talk about being a mediator, and being able to explain something from one society to another, or one culture to another, then I am thinking of somebody being in a third space, being in an intercultural space. You can call it a third space if you like. In the third space, you don't need a native speaker language competence. What's important in this third space or this intercultural space is that we remember that the learner is not to be compared to a native speaker in either space/culture one or in space/culture two.

The question seems to refer to Vygotsky's work which is a theory of learning. The idea that you should always start from where the learner is and to add something new to build upon what they already knew. That is a simplification of Vygotsky to say the least. But in a way, that's just a description of a good teaching that you have to try to know where your learners are. Like in these lectures, I have had to guess where you are, and I guess that you know a lot about language competence. You know a lot about assessments of language and communicative competence. I then referred to that as a means of saying 'I assume you know about language assessment. And now let's think about how we can use what you know as a basis for thinking further about intercultural assessment or teaching'.

Questioner 2: I have a question. I'd like to know: In your research do you have any self-assessment tools that the students can use in classroom? Thank you. I'd like to hear the introduction about the tools used in classroom for students' self-assessment. Thanks.

Michael Byram: I'm afraid the short answer is 'no'. The short answer will have to be 'no' in the sense that the assessment depends on what you are teaching. What could exist but to my knowledge does not exist is a means of saying, like the

提问人 2：我想请问一个问题。我想知道，在你们的研究当中有没有一些课堂教学中学生可以使用的自我评价工具？我想听听关于这些自我评价工具的介绍，谢谢。

Michael Byram：这个恐怕是没有的。之所以没有，是因为评价的依据是你的教学内容。就我所知，这种工具可以是类似于《跨文化经历自传》里提出的一系列问题，这些问题能够帮助老师和学生认识到自己的教学和学习现状。本该有这样的工具，但是现在还没有，就我所知现在还没有这样的工具。你自己必须要和其他老师一起开发这样的工具。通常来说，正式开始上课之前，你都会告诉学生本节课的目标是什么，现在很多课本也都是这么安排的，每一章的开头就开宗明义："本章结束时你将学到……"，有时也会写"你将能够……"。学生可以在自我评价中不断参照这些目标，自问"我能达到目标的要求吗？"然后他们可以建立个人档案，记录或描述自己做过的事情。但我不知道有什么现成的工具可以直接拿来用，你必须得自己创造。

提问人 3：谢谢 Michael Byram 教授，今天您讲的可能更多的是老师如何评估学生的跨文化交际能力，我的问题是如何评估第二语言教师，具体地说，如何评价我们国际汉语教师的跨文化交际能力？对这个庞大的群体，有没有一种较为可靠的评估方法？

Michael Byram：简单来说，还是没有。包括中国在内的很多国家都以对跨文化能力感兴趣的教师作为对象开展了不少研究。研究表明，在很多情况下教师都是愿意教授跨文化能力的。尽管大家教的是汉语，大家肯定也都知道中国的英语课程已经把跨文化能力作为必学的内容，至少是推荐学习的内容，老师们也很有兴趣教授这方面的知识。但是研究也表明，大部分老师对跨文化能力的概念不是特别清楚。研究发现，很多老师都认为，教授跨文化能力其实就是教"是什么的知识"，仅此而已。所以从这个角度来说，老师们对这些概念的理解还有待进一步加强。

这类研究中的教师知道，跨文化能力可以通过我前面提到的贝内特和其他人发明的测试方法进行检测。但老师是否应该接受这样的跨文化能力考

Autobiography, here is a series of questions which will help the teacher and the learner to think about what they have been teaching and learning. I don't know of a tool which already exists for that. It's something that you would have to make for yourself together with other teachers. I think you have to work together with other teachers. It's part of what is usual in teaching that before you begin your lessons, you tell your learners what your objectives are. And in many textbooks you find this today. You find it in the beginning of a chapter the textbook will say 'by the end of this chapter, you will 'know that' and sometimes 'you will be able to do…'. Students can constantly refer to this in self-assessment, asking themselves 'Can I do what it says is the objective?' Then they can produce a profile, that is, they keep a diary or a profile of what they are doing. But I don't know anything which is ready made. It's something you would have to make for yourself.

Questioner 3: Thank you, Professor Michael Byram. Firstly, thank you very much. What you have talked about today is perhaps mainly about how a teacher evaluates the students' intercultural communicative competence, and my question is how we evaluate a L2 teacher, to be specific, how we can evaluate the intercultural communicative competence of a Chinese teacher who teaches Chinese language to the speakers of other languages. Is there a fairly reliable approach to better evaluate such a big group of people?

Michael Byram: Again I think I have to say the short answer is 'no'. There is quite a lot of research, including research in China, about teachers interested in intercultural competence. So we know from research that teachers have a willingness in many cases to teach intercultural competence. Although you are teachers of Chinese, I'm sure you know that in the curriculum of teaching English in China, intercultural competence is a requirement, or is a recommendation at least, and teachers are interested in doing so. But we also know from research that most teachers do not have a clear understanding of what intercultural competence is. Most teachers in the research think that to teach intercultural competence is to teach 'knowledge that' and only 'knowledge that'. So in that sense we know from research that teachers' understanding of these ideas still needs to be developed.

Teachers in this kind of research know intercultural competence could be tested using the kind of test that I described from Bennett and other people. But whether this should be done is something that needs to be decided within an education system as a whole rather than by an individual teacher. An education system would have to decide, whether teachers will have language competence

试并不是由老师自己决定的，而是由整个教育系统决定的。教育系统要决定
老师是否应该参加语言能力测试和跨文化能力测试。这也许是可能的，但我
不知道在哪些国家有这种考试。现在立刻就开始这类考试未必是个好主意，
因为这可能会给教师带来不安。我们都还处在学习的过程中，我来这里就是
为了帮助大家了解这些问题，而不是指出大家在实践中的缺憾。

提问人 4：可能是有些老师还没有接受这样的观念，事实上我觉得您的
这套理论需要进行本地化，要结合中国情况，具有中国特色才行。为什么？
我们的汉语国际教育有一个指挥棒，HSK，就像英语教育里也有指挥棒一样。
如果我把孩子送到您的班，按照您的方式教学，我觉得很成功；但是他要参
加专业的考试，可能就拿不到满意的分数，换句话说就是不能毕业。这样作
为一个家长，我就需要三思而行。老师和学生要评估，家长也需要思考这样
做合不合适。因此我的问题是，北外作为我们外语教学的大本营、桥头堡，
它能否在 HSK 考试里面融入跨文化交际能力这个指挥棒？教授能不能给我
们一个建议。

Michael Byram：首先我要说，中国并不是特例。我想无论到哪里都会
遇到您所说的这种问题。我所说的高风险考试就是这个意思。我们都知道考
试很重要，它们甚至在国家之间的互相比较中变得愈发重要了。负责考试的
人知道他们不能只想测试，而不管其他形式的跨文化能力评价，但是他们不
知道该做什么，也不知道如何去做。如果问我的话我就会说，我可以发明出
一些新的形式来，但这不是仅仅一支笔和一张纸，或者是一台可以联网的计
算机就可以完成的，它需要的远远不止这些。它所花费的也远远不止这些。
考官要花时间观察人们的行为，这是要花不少钱的。目前为止我还找不到成
本很低的方法来做这件事情。

让我们来比较一下文学的教学。学生们在学校里学习中国文学，然后参
加考试，拿到证书。如果我们想分析一下在这个过程中都发生了什么，我们
就会说，可能这些考试的有效性和可靠性是有问题的。但实际上文学考试一
直都有，我很久很久之前也参加过文学方面的考试，大学发给我的证书上表
明我的文学学得还不错。但是如果你要以科学的方法去考查文学考试的方式

tests, they should also have intercultural competence tests. It would be possible, but I don't know anywhere where it has been done. It might not be a good idea for this kind of testing to be done immediately, because that might lead to insecurity among teachers. We all have to learn. What I am trying to do here is to help you to learn about these things rather than to say you don't know how to do it.

Questioner 4: Perhaps some teachers have not adopted these notions yet. In fact, in China, I think your theory might need undergo a process of localisation, to develop a theory with Chinese characteristics through integration. The reason for this is that Teaching Chinese to the Speakers of Other Languages is guided by the baton HSK, like the baton of testing in English teaching. If I send my child to your class to be taught in your way, I think it is a success; but if he needs to sit on the examination, his score may not be satisfactory. In other words, he may not graduate. Then as a parent, I need a second thought. Both teachers and students need do evaluations, as well as parents, to think about whether this is suitable. So my question for the professor is, could you give us advice as to whether the baton of intercultural communicative competence should be introduced into HSK test, since BFSU is the stronghold taking the lead in foreign language education in China.

Michael Byram: First of all, China is not special. The same question arises wherever you go. That's what I meant by high-stakes testing. We are all aware that examinations are important. They are becoming more and more important as countries compare each other on tests. Examination people know that they would like to include testing rather than other kinds of assessment of intercultural competence, but they don't know what to do, and they don't know how to do it. If I were asked I would say I can invent something. But it will require not just a paper and a pencil as it were or even a computer on the Internet, but something more than that. And it will cost more. It will be that examiners will have to spend time observing people doing things, and that costs money. At the moment I cannot find a cheap way of doing this.

Let us compare with the teaching of literature. Learners at school study Chinese literature and they do examinations, which give certificates. If one were to analyse what is happening in that process, we will begin to say there may be some problems in the validity and reliability in the examinations. But literature examinations have existed forever, even I did the literature examinations a long time ago, and I was given a certificate from my university to say that I was good at literature. Yet if we were to examine in a scientific way how literature studies are

及其授予证书的标准，你就会发现，这整个过程都不太令人满意。有人可能会说，我们可以像文学考试那样，让学生在跨文化能力考试中写一篇文章，然后颁给他们证书。但如今想要在考试系统中引入新的理念，你必须要满足更高的科学标准，这样做显然是行不通的。

我也可以稍微乐观一点地看待这个问题。从理论和实际上我们都知道，学习和提高语言能力最好的途径就是让学生在重要、严肃的场合使用这门语言，这对他们的认知能力要求很高，并且最终可以通过考试的形式得到检测。在美国，有一种以内容为基础的教学 (CBI)，无论是孩子，还是大学生，他们都是通过外语来学习课程内容的。欧洲有类似的教学方法，只是叫法有点不同，我们称其为内容语言综合学习 (CLIL)。用外语来教授其他科目，其实是外语教学的最佳方式。很多研究都已证明该方法虽不完美，但是的确有效。我刚才讲的案例就是在外语课堂上进行以内容为基础的教学。换句话说，在外语课堂中，我们是在教其他学科而不是语言本身。我们的教学对象可能是未来的民族志学者、科学家，他们可能会去分析数据。所以学习者关注的是内容，并且要用外语来分析这些内容。这意味着他们的外语水平在不断提高。如果你接受这项研究及其成果，作为老师——我们必须说服家长——至少能在一段时间内实施这样的教学模式，只有这样学生的语言能力才会提高，他们在语言测试中才能取得更好的成绩。从这个角度来看，考试就有其积极的意义了。

提问人 5：您提到"语言文化"这个概念，那么这个词的形态学结构是怎样的？因为这个词涉及"语言"和"文化"两者间的关系，从形态学上讲，在"语言文化"这个词中，"文化"是核心部分，而"语言"则是一个形容词。从这个意义上讲，它就对语言课程的设计产生了影响，反之亦然。如果"语言"是这个词的核心部分，"文化"是形容词，那么重心就变成了如何将文化因素嵌入语言课程了。但是您所说的"语言文化"是指把语言学的元素融入文化教学中。但是课程本身是语言教学课。那就意味着语言课程要么是文化本位要么是语言本位。实际上我们有另外一个术语，叫"文化语言学"。

Michael Byram：很高兴你问了这个问题。首先，在我刚才给大家举的四个例子中，有三个例子是在语言课堂上完成的项目。我要强调这些项目是

examined and certificates given, today it would not be satisfactory. One could argue we could do the same for intercultural competence as for literature examinations and ask students to write an essay and then give them a certificate. But today when you try to introduce new ideas of examination, you have to meet higher scientific standards, and this approach would not be acceptable.

Let me be a little more positive. We know from theory and practice that the best way to learn and improve your language competence which will be tested in an examination, is to get learners to use their language in serious and important ways, cognitively demanding ways. In the US they have content-based instruction (CBI) where children and university students learn other subjects through foreign languages. And in Europe we have the same but call it Content and Language Integrated Learning (CLIL). This is the best way to teach a foreign language, and to use it to teach another subject. There is plenty of research to say that it is working, not perfect but working. What we are doing in the examples I have described, is to do content-based instruction in the foreign language classroom. In other words, in the foreign language classroom, we are teaching another subject. The subject we are teaching is to be an ethnographer, to be a scientist, to do analysis of data. So the learners are focusing upon content and having to use their foreign language to do that. That means their foreign languages are improving. If you accept that research and those results, as a teacher – and we have to persuade the parents – and carry out this kind of teaching for some of the time at least, then learners' language competence will improve, and they will do better in their language examinations. That's a more positive way of thinking about examinations.

Questioner 5: You use a term languaculture. So what kind of the morphological structure of this term? Because it's related to the relationship between language and culture. Morphologically speaking, languaculture means culture is the head, and the language is an adjective. In that sense, it's related to how to design the curriculum of the language class, and vice versa. If the langua is the head, culture is an adjective, then it should become how we incorporate into cultural components into language class. But the term you use 'languaculture' means we incorporate linguistic components into culture class. But the curriculum design is a language class. So that means language class is culture prominent based or language prominent based. Actually we have another term you know. Cultural linguistics.

Michael Byram: I am very glad you asked that question. First of all, of these four examples, three are projects, projects within a language class. So it's important

延续了几周时间的，并且涉及了好几堂课。但是，在这个学年的剩余时间里，在其他课堂上，老师是在进行"现代的"交际型语言教学，而不是"传统的"语言教学。课程主要还是以语言教学为主。但是，因为即使是在纯粹的语言教学中教师也会考虑到文化的问题，所以他们会更关注语义，而传统的教学里他们只会关注语法和字典词义。我不是说这些例子中的实践活动就是这些老师所做的全部。他们仍旧是语言老师。所以我也不能确定他们究竟是语言文化教师还是文化语言教师，但即使他们在做项目的时候他们依然是语言教师。他们在挖掘学生的能力。他们努力让学生对语言本身有更深刻的理解。比如，如果我们回想老师教授关于圣诞贺卡的课程时，我们会发现过去这个主题的课程通常放在12月的圣诞节前后——大多数教师都会这么选择——这使得课程变得有趣而轻松，充满了异国情调。但在保加利亚的这堂英语课结束之后，学生不但理解了什么是"圣诞贺卡"，还理解了"圣诞贺卡"这个词不能被翻译成保加利亚语——至少不能简单地按照字面意思来一一对应——因为就是这么张简单的贺卡，它在英国的含义和在保加利亚的含义已经不同了。这就是一个很简单的例子。

Michael Byram：刚才在茶歇时有人问了我一些有趣的问题，和大家分享一下。有人问我如何选择要讲的话题。有人问我在自己上课的时候，如何将跨文化交际能力等融入语言课程。我想先回答一下第二个问题，也当作是对主持人所提问题的回应。我的建议是，在常规的语言教学课上，我们可以时常让学生做一些项目，我给大家举的例子都是关于做项目的，项目可长可短，有的只需要几节课，有的需要好几周的课，这取决于课程的安排。因此，你一年可能只做一个项目，也可能做两个或三个项目，这主要取决于学校给老师安排的课程情况。

其次，我如何来选择话题，这同样也取决于你们。但从我给大家举的这几个例子来看，如果我们回想美国的学生用西班牙语学习"水果"这个主题的课程时会发现，"水果"这个话题其实是给定的。它是这门课的一个常规话题，每年都会讲到。所以并不是老师选择话题，而是这个话题对老师和学生来说，是个固定话题。老师要做的是把传统课堂里对水果的探讨变成一个项目，让学生自己来收集数据等等。在保加利亚，教圣诞贺卡的老师自由度

to emphasise that these projects took place over several weeks over a number of lessons. But in other parts of the year or of the course, the teachers were teaching what I would call 'modern' communicative language teaching, not 'traditional' language teaching. Lessons were still dominated by langua, by language. However, because the teachers are also thinking about culture, even in the language dominant lessons, they will be paying more attention to semantics, whereas traditionally they will be focusing upon grammar and the dictionary meanings. I am not saying that these examples are, in the practice of the teachers I gave you, all that they do. They continue to be language teachers. So I am not sure whether they are languaculture teachers or culture language teachers, but even when the teachers are doing their projects, they are still language teachers. They are developing the competence of their learners. They are developing their learners' understanding of language in a deeper way. For example, if we think about the teacher teaching Christmas cards, in the past when she taught 'Christmas' in December – as many teachers do – it was seen as something exotic, and just a leisure lesson. But in this case from Bulgaria, at the end of the lesson, the learners understood what a Christmas card was, and understood that the phrase 'Christmas card' cannot be translated into Bulgarian – not in a straightforward or simple way – because the meanings of that simple card in England are different from the connotations in Bulgaria. That's just a simple example.

Michael Byram: There were some interesting questions during the break, one of which I would like to share with everybody. Somebody asked me how do I choose the topics that I want to address. Somebody asked me what do I do in my own language classroom to integrate intercultural competence and so on with my language teaching. Let me take the second question, as I said in response to our chairman's question. What I am suggesting is that during your ordinary course of teaching, from time to time, that the learners do a project. All the examples I have been giving you have been projects. Some longer, some shorter, some just a few lessons, some a few weeks, depending on the way the course works. Therefore, maybe you do one project, maybe you do two projects, maybe you do three projects in a year. It depends on you as the teacher on your situation in your institution.

Secondly, how do I choose those topics for those lessons. Again it depends upon you. But if I take the examples I gave you so far, then if we think about the project where the students in the US were doing 'fruit' in Spanish. The topic 'fruit' was given. It was a part of the curriculum, something they do every year. So the teacher did not choose the topic. The topic was chosen for the teacher and the learners. What she did was to change a traditional course about fruit into a

相对大一些。她可以选择她想讲的话题，因为当时是 12 月，所以她就选择了圣诞节这个话题。而王丽虹给出的关于筷子的例子则是直接源于教材的，所以我们的理念应该是从课本中找到一些灵感，然后把它变成一个项目。对于丹麦这个例子，话题则是来源于学生自身。学生说他们想要了解更多丹麦的情况。而在你们的情境中，你们的学生可能会说他们想了解更多中国的情况。之后我还会给大家举一个例子，话题来自于新闻报道。所以选择某一个话题的原因是多种多样的。从某种意义上讲，选择什么话题其实并不重要，因为你的目标是让学生学习如何做，获得"怎么做的知识"，所以你采用怎样的话题来达成这些目标就无关紧要了。

project for the learners, where they collected data and so on. In the case of the Bulgarian teacher teaching Christmas, she had a little more freedom. She could decide what topic she wanted and because it was December she chose something to do with Christmas. In the case of the chopsticks example that Lihong gave, that is something which is in the textbook, the idea is you take something from the textbook and change it into a project. In the example from Denmark, the topic came from the learners. The learners say 'we want to know more about something in Denmark', or in your case, your learners might say 'we want to know more about something particular in China'. In another example which I will give in a moment, the focus will be a subject which was topical, it was in the news. So there are different reasons. In a way it doesn't matter what the topic is, because the objectives are objectives of learning how to do things, acquiring knowledge how. It doesn't matter what you focus upon in order to achieve these.

批判性思维与人文主义目标

介绍

今天最后一节讲座，我想请大家回顾一下大学英语这门课程的教学大纲。大纲中有非常明确的目标，既包括工具性的语言教学目标，也涵盖人文性的，或是"语言文化"的语言教学目标。作为语言教师，无论是传授知识还是教学生成为更优秀、更成熟的人，从而能够理解自己国家的文化和别国的文化，我们的教学都应该是对学习者有益的。

为了做到这一点，需要用到探索、阐释及建立关联的技能，这些都是工具性的目标，在学习跨文化交际能力的过程中，这些技能都用得上。这些技能之所以能够在今后派上用场，是因为当下教师不可能在课堂上面面俱到地传授知识。但在跨文化交际能力中还存在人文性的目标，即努力培养学生的

Humanistic and Critical Approaches

Introduction

In my final session, I want to remind you of the *College English Teaching Syllabus*. This is a very clear statement. There are both instrumental and humanistic purposes for language teaching, or 'languaculture' teaching. What we do as language teachers should be useful to the learners, but it should also educate them and make them better people, more complex and sophisticated people who can understand other countries and their own.

In the approach I have suggested for doing this, there are skills of discovery, of interpreting and of relating which are instrumental in the sense that if learners are taught intercultural competence, it will be useful for them in the future. These are useful skills for the future because it is not possible to teach learners all they know in the classroom, in the present. But there are also humanistic dimensions to intercultural competence. That is, we are trying to develop our learners' curiosity or openness, and their critical cultural awareness. Now I want to focus more upon the humanistic and the critical element of language teaching.

REMINDER

College English Teaching Syllabus 2015

* College English course is part of the humanity (liberal arts) education and it represents both instrumental and humanistic features.

* 4.2.3 Intercultural communication course
Intercultural communication course aims at intercultural education, helps students understand the different outlook, values, thinking modes between China and other countries, cultivate the students' intercultural awareness, improve their social linguistic and intercultural communication ability.

* [instrumental = skills of discovery AND interpreting/relating (AND knowledge)]
* [humanistic = openness/curiosity AND critical cultural awareness]

'To study without thinking is futile. To think without studying is dangerous' – The Analects 2.15

* Part 1: The teacher's dilemma

* Part 2: Intercultural Competence and Mediation

* Part 3: 'Critical Thinking' and 'Action in the Community'

* Part 4: Language Teaching in Society – the European Example

好奇心、开放的心态以及文化批判的意识。现在，我想把重心放在语言教学中的人文主义和批判性元素上。

这里分成四个部分，而且我要用孔子的话作为引言，他曾说过，"学而不思则罔，思而不学则殆"，我希望可以像孔子说的那样，在学习中把学与思有机地结合起来。

首先，我会详细谈一谈"教师的困境"这一问题。其次，我会讨论跨文化交际和沟通协调的能力。上一讲里，我用了"协调沟通"这个词，我想要进一步澄清这个概念。第三，我想讲一讲"批判性思维"和"在社区中行动"这两个概念。最后，我会把语言教学放入更宽广的社会语境中，举一些欧洲语言教学的例子供大家参考。

教师的困境

作为语言教师，从教授语法和词汇等角度来讲，他完全可以是中立的，但作为语言文化教师，他就不可能是中立的。你们中的一些人可能会去其他国家教汉语，作为一个生活在异国他乡的老师和学生，你不可能是中立的。

The teacher's dilemma – as teacher and learner...

- As teacher = neutral language teacher or languaculture teacher...

- As learner = being a teacher-learner in a foreign country...

正如我在前几讲也引用过的贝内特（1993）所言，当你发现自己既是教师又是学生时，就会对自己所处的环境产生反应。但不管你是在国外还是国内教汉语，教师的困境都是一样的：我希望自己的学生在贝内特的尺度表里达到什么阶段？我希望学生能够通过学习成为一个完全不同的人，彻底融入中国的文化？又或者我希望学生走向尺度表里的另一个极端，抵制一切异文化？

我们肯定不希望学生抵制外来文化，贝内特尺度表里描述的前三种状态

I have four parts to this, and I would quote Confucius as my introduction since he says, 'To study without thinking is futile; to think without studying is dangerous'. I hope we can combine thinking and studying in a way that Confucius would approve.

First of all, I will talk more about what I call the teacher's dilemma. Secondly, I will consider intercultural competence and mediation. I have used the word 'mediation' in a previous lecture and I want to make it clearer. Thirdly, I will introduce the notions of 'critical thinking' and 'action in the community'. Finally, for your information, I will talk about what we are doing in Europe, with respect to language teaching in the wider society.

The Teacher's Dilemma

As a teacher of language, in the sense of grammar and vocabulary and so on, one can be neutral, but as a teacher of languaculture, the teacher cannot be neutral. If you are going to another country to teach Chinese as some of you maybe, as a teacher and learner in a foreign country, you cannot be neutral.

As Bennett (1993) whom I quoted in an earlier lecture, says, you will respond to the environment in which you will find yourself as a teacher-learner. However, whether you are in a foreign country or teaching Chinese in China, the teacher's dilemma is the same: How far do I want my learners to go on Bennett's scale? Do I want my learners to go all the way to become a different person, integrating into Chinese culture? Or do I want them to remain on the left hand side and resist anything which is different?

I'm sure that we do not want our learners to remain on the left hand side, in the first three categories, which are still ethnocentric when they are still thinking about other countries from their own perspectives. But perhaps we do not want them to become completely different, to give up their identity as Vietnamese, Americans whatever, and become Chinese. I certainly did not want my learners to become French when I was teaching them French. Somewhere in the middle

Developmental Model of Intercultural Sensitivity - Bennett

• Denial →Defence → Minimisation →Acceptance → Adaptation → Integration

Teacher's dilemma:
- How far do I want my learners to go?

Teacher-learner's dilemma (when teaching Chinese in another country):
- How far do I want to go?

仍然是具有民族中心性的，仍然是从自己的角度看别国的文化。但是我们可能也不希望学生完全成为另外一个人，完全放弃自己越南人、美国人或是任何国家的人的身份，而变成中国人。在我教学生法语时，我肯定不想让他们变成法国人。介于两者之间才是我们想要的结果。作为教师，我们要根据自己所处的位置和教授的对象来考虑这些问题。

同时，既作为老师也作为学生的我们也应该考虑一下自己所处的位置。比如，假设你在美国教汉语，那么你就要思考一下，按照贝内特的度量表，作为学生的你要走多远？当我们身处异国他乡时，这一度量表可以帮助我们思索自身的处境。我们是如何对异文化做出反应的？从完全抵制到完全接受，我们究竟能走多远？我不会回答这些问题。这些需要每位教师自己来找答案。但这是教师困境的另一个侧面，需要我们进一步思考。

文化与双文化的交际能力和教师的困境

我们可以通过分析文化和双文化能力的不同来重新解读一下教师的困境。

文化能力就是在大多情况下按照某人所属群体的行为方式去行事。中国人在大部分情况下会像其他中国人那样做事情，大多数情况下中国人彼此之间也有很多相似之处，当然这不是说所有人都一样，而是大部分情况下大部分的人都有相似性。从这个意义上讲，大家都具备中国的文化能力，而我具备的则是英国的文化能力。这是一种简单的情况。

还有一些人是双文化的。换句话说，他们被两个不同但平行且类似的群体认同，并按照这两个群体的行为准则来行事。比如，你很有可能认为自己是中国人，会按照中国文化的要求来行事，同时认为自己也是美国人，按照美国文化的习惯来行事。所以有人称自己为美籍华人，这些人就是双文化的，他们可以生活在两种文化中，认同于两种文化并按照两种文化的不同要求来行动。如果我们回过头来看贝内特的度量表，那些走到了最右边的人可以成为双文化者。他们一方面保留了中国人的身份，按照中国文化来做事，另一方面他们也可以成为美国人或美籍华人，到了英国他们也可以既是中国人也是英国人。我在大学时的一个秘书就是这样，她是中国人，在家里她仍是中国人，但在办公室里她的语言和文化习惯都是英国式的。

is where we want them to be. We as teachers have to think about these issues according to where and whom we teach.

We also have to think about our own position as teacher-learners. For example, if you are in America teaching Chinese, there is a question of how far you want to go along the scale as a learner. Bennett's scale helps us to think about ourselves when we are in a different country. How are we reacting? How far do we want to move from left to right? I am not going to answer the questions. These are questions that every teacher has to answer for themselves. But it's another aspect of the dilemma. It's a question which we have to think about.

Cultural and bicultural competence – and the teacher's dilemma

We can consider the same issues from a different perspective by analysing the difference between cultural and bicultural competence.

Cultural competence refers to enacting – most of the time – the behaviours of groups one belongs to. Chinese people do what other Chinese people do most of the time, and are like other Chinese people most of the time, but of course not everybody is identical. In that sense, a Chinese person has Chinese cultural competence. In my case, I have English cultural competence. That's the simple situation.

Some people are also bicultural. In other words, they can enact the behaviours and identify with two different but parallel and similar groups. It is possible to identify yourself as Chinese and to 'do' Chinese culture, but at the same time to identify as American and to 'do' American culture, for example. There are therefore people who call themselves Chinese-Americans, who are bicultural, who can live, be and 'do' in two different cultural groups. If we return to Bennett's scale, then someone who moves all the way to the right hand side can become bicultural. They can keep their Chinese identity, 'do' Chinese culture, but they can become Americans or Chinese-Americans or in Britain, they can be both Chinese and British. One of my secretaries at university was exactly like that. She was Chinese. In the office she was English both in language and culture, but at home she was Chinese.

The teacher's dilemma, to repeat, is: Do I want my students wherever they come from to do the same as Chinese, to be the same as Chinese? Do I want them to move all the way to the right hand side on Bennett's continuum? To become bicultural? My answer would be no, but every teacher has to decide for themselves how they answer this question.

For it is possible for learners to move part of the way, to learn the polite

Cultural and Bicultural Competence

- Cultural competence – ability to do (most of the time) 'behaviours, values and beliefs of group X'
  - = Chinese person does what other Chinese do/is the same as other Chinese

- Bicultural competence – ability to do... in groups X and Y when X and Y are 'the same'
  - = Chinese person can do (and be) same as 'Chinese' **and** same as 'American'/ 'French'/ 'Japanese', etc,

- Teacher's dilemma – Do I want my US/Vietnamese learners to do the same as Chinese? To be the same?

再重复一遍，教师的困境就是：无论自己的学生来自哪个国家，我希望他们都像中国人一样行事吗？最终都变得和中国人一样吗？我希望他们一直走到贝内特度量表的最右端，完全接受外来的文化吗？成为一个双文化者？我的回答是否定的，但每个教师都有权决定自己的答案。

学生能做到的是，努力去学习一些礼貌用语，学习大部分中国人在大多数情况下是如何打招呼的。这是文化行为的表层，学生是可以学会的，他们可以在不变成中国人的情况下而做到模仿。这可能就是你希望学生在语言层面（学习如何打招呼）和文化层面（模仿某些行为，从而懂得他国文化的信仰理念）上能够达到的水平。

比如，在一些国家，人们相信教师拥有惩罚的权利。这就是某些国家的信仰理念。在英国，过去人们也是这样认为的，但现在已经完全不是这样了，教师无权再对学生进行体罚或是其他形式的惩罚。不管效果如何，这就是现状，是主流的观念。虽然不是每个人都认同，但大部分人在大部分情况下都认同这一观点。如果这名教师去了另外一个国家，就像我若干年前那样，并且发现这个国家的主流观点和自己国家的大相径庭，问题就出现了：我是应该接受新的观念？还是单纯地尝试去理解别人的理念，同时与其保持距离？

换句话说，作为老师我希望我的学生**接受**他人的信仰，还是仅仅**理解**并学会**阐释**这种信仰？还是我想更进一步，鼓励我的学生完全吸收另一种文化的价值观？比如中国的英语教师可能主要关注美国或英国的价值理念，他们会发现，这两个国家有一种主流的理念认为，年轻就是好。在我所处的社会中年长就没那么好了，但在中国，年长是好的。那么对中国的英语教师而言

language, to 'do' the greetings that most Chinese 'do' most of the time do. That is the surface level of cultural behaviour, and it is possible to imitate Chinese behaviour without becoming Chinese. That may be something you want your learners to do, both linguistically – learning the greetings – and culturally you may want them to imitate aspects of behaviour, and to understand the beliefs of another culture.

For example, in some countries, people believe that the teacher should have the right to punish. That's a belief in some countries. In Britain, although it used to be so, that is no longer the case, and teachers are not allowed to punish, either physically or in other way. For better or for worse, that's the way it is. That's the dominant belief. Not everybody, but most people most of the time believe that. If teachers then go to another country as I did a long time ago and find a different belief, the question arises: Do I adapt to a new belief or do I simply try to understand what other people believe, without adapting to it?

In other words, do I as a teacher want my learners to *adapt* to other people's beliefs or simply to *understand* and be able to *explain* them? Or do I want to go even further and encourage my learners to take on the values of another culture? For example teachers of English in China who might be focusing upon the US or Britain, will find that one of the dominant values is that to be young is good. To be old is not so good in my society, whereas to be old is good in China. The question then is for the teacher of English in China: Do I want my learners to change their values? Do I want my Chinese learners to change their values to those of the US or Britain, the values of most people most of the time? My answer would again be 'no'. I don't want my learners to change their existing values and take on new values, but I do want them to understand how other people's values work, and to be able to compare and contrast. They should be able to ask themselves: Why do I as a Chinese person have a certain value of which being old is good? Why do I think that? What is it in the way that I was brought up which makes me think that? Should I be more conscious of the values that I have and that I think are good? Since 'good' is an empty word signifying only 'I approve', learners have to

> Examples
> Culture = values, beliefs and behaviours
>
> * Behaviours, e.g. Politeness: most but not all (Chinese/ English/ Japanese, etc.) greet each other by saying...
> * Beliefs, e.g. most but not all... believe that teachers should have rights to punish ...
> * Values, e.g. most but not all... give priority/ admire young people's ways of life
>
> * Teacher's dilemma = Do I want my US/Vietnamese learners to behave/believe/ value the same as Chinese?

问题就是：我想要我的学生改变他们的价值观吗？我想让我的学生按照英美国家大多数人在大多数情况下所遵循的价值观来生活吗？对此问题，我的回答依然是否定的。我不希望他们改变已有的价值理念，建立新的价值观。但是我确实希望他们能够了解其他国家人的价值观是如何运作的，从而进行对比和比较。他们应该学会自问：作为中国人，为什么我们的某些价值理念宣扬的是年长之美？我为什么会认同这一观点？在我成长的环境中有哪些因素促使我产生这样的想法？我应该更加在意自己现有的价值观和那些我认为好的理念吗？由于"好"是个很空洞的词，只表明"我赞许"，所以学生要自问："为什么我觉得某件事是好的，为什么我会赞许它？"对比和比较其他文化中的价值观可以帮助学生对自己的本国文化及价值观产生更深刻的理解。

身份与教师的困境

还有一个类似的问题是身份问题。如果你教的是语言能力——因为翻译是不完美的——因此尽可能让学生用外语来表达想用本国语言表达的意思，那么你就是处于中立位置的。你的教学对学生的身份不会产生什么影响，研究结果已经证实了这一点。有的研究是关于学习者在多大程度上由于语言学习改变了自己的身份——比如一个英国人学法语或是一个中国人学英语——研究表明：如果你只教语言，就不会对学生的身份产生影响，教学始终是中性的。但是如果你教的是跨文化能力，是关于另一种文化中信仰和其他理念的"知识"，这就会对学生的身份产生影响。

比方说，我在中国经常被问到的一个问题就是：教授英语会不会改变中国人？这个是困扰许多中国教师和家长的问题。我的回答则是，如果你只教语言的话是没有问题的，但如果教的是语言文化，那就会出现一定的风险，这也是困境的另一个侧面。但是学生是否能意识到自己所发生的改变是取决于教师的。学生需要明白，他们在学习另外一个国家的文化并将其与中国文化对比和比较时，不应该产生中国更好或者比如美国更好这样的结论。对比与比较的核心在于让学生把两国的情况平等地放在一起，从而更好地了解这两种文化。不是说"美国更好，我们在好莱坞看到的一切都更好"或相反。比较的目的是为了理解。如果这就是你所强调的内容，那么便不会对学生的身份产生影响，但这确实是一个我们不得不考虑的困境。

ask themselves: 'Why do I think that something is good? Why do I approve of it?' Comparing and contrasting other values in other societies helps learners to become more conscious of their own values in their own society.

Identity and the teacher's dilemma

A similar question arises with respect to identity. If you teach language competence, that is the ability to use a foreign language to express what learners would say in their own language – as far as that is possible since translation is never perfect – then you are being neutral. There is going to be no effect upon your learners' identity. The research shows that that is the case. For there is research about to what extent learners' identity changes as a result of language learning – let's say English people learning French or Chinese people learning English – and the research shows that if you simply teach language competence, then it will have no effect upon identities; teaching remains neutral. If you teach intercultural competence, and you simply teach 'knowledge about' the beliefs and other facts in another culture, then there could be an effect upon identity.

For example, on a number of cases in China, I have been asked by people: Is teaching English changing Chinese people? That's a worry that I have heard from Chinese people, from teachers and from parents. My answer is that as long as students are simply learning the language, there is no danger. When we are teaching languaculture, then there is a risk, another aspect of the dilemma. But it's up to the teacher to make the learners aware of what's happening to them. They need to understand, when they are learning about another country or culture, and comparing and contrasting with China, that it is not a matter of saying that China is better, or USA for example is better. Comparison and contrast is a matter of putting things side by side, in order to understand each one better. Not to say 'USA is better, everything we see from Hollywood is better'. Or vice versa. It's a matter of comparing in order to understand. If that is your emphasis, then there will be no effect upon identity. But it is a dilemma which we

---

Teacher's dilemma – my answer

- NOT **Bicultural** competence: Vietnamese and Chinese = have culture of both (most but not all) Vietnamese **and** Chinese = 2 identities
- BUT **Intercultural** competence: know that/how (most but not all) Americans believe value and behave **AND** same for Chinese (but remain Chinese in identity) AND be able to 'mediate'

- MEDIATION examples:
  - history teachers mediate the past for their learners...
  - Chinese teachers mediate Chinese culture for their learners...

最后作为总结，我对这一困境的回答就是，我不会让我的学生去做双文化人。我从不想让学法语的英国孩子变成法国人，变成有双重文化背景的人。我想做的是让我的学生获得一种新的能力，而不是新的身份。他们应该学会沟通协调，以他人的目光来审视自身。

跨文化交际能力与中介

中介是一个非常有意思的词。教师就是中介。比方说，想想中学或大学时，你的历史老师是如何给作为学生的你上课的吧。他们试图告诉你中国或其他国家的人们在不同的历史时段里都是如何生活的。最好的历史老师会把学生带入另外一个时空，让其短暂地感受一下生活在另一个时代是怎样的情景。在这个过程中，学生的身份并没有改变，他们只是从一个不同的时间维度去看待这个世界。

在语言教学中也应该这样做，汉语老师应该帮助学生理解中国的文化和中国人的处事方式，从而让学生反思自身。这就是中介的一个方面。下面这幅简图将帮助我们进一步理解中介的概念。

左边是一个中国人，可能是老师、母亲、父亲或其他任何一种身份。右边比方说是一个美国人，可能也是老师、母亲、父亲、足球运动员等其他各种身份。大家可以看到在他们的头上，显示的是作为中国人、教师和母亲等各自的文化认同，每一种不同的身份使他们归属于不同的社会群体。中国人主要是在学校里学习中国的文化。教师则是在教师培训课程中意识到教师文化的存在。对于右边的美国人而言情况也是如此。

而处在中间的则是一个成功的学习者，他知道如何协调和沟通两种文化，能够把一种文化阐释给另一种文化中的人。让我们以教师文化为例，中介能够向一个美国人，比如 Richard Smith，来解释中国老师王辉（音）头脑中的教师文化。中介能够处在中间的位置并解释："在中国，教学的理念是……；而在美国，教学理念则是……"为了让 Richard Smith 理解中国式思维和教学理念，他需要比较两种文化（美国与中国）中教学理念的异同。中介站在"第三空间"里，跨越两个民族的文化，这种文化既非完全中国的也非完全美国的。

丽虹曾讲过一个真实的例子，她在美国的孔子学院教书时注意到，那里

have to consider.

As a means of summing up, my own answer to the dilemma is not to try to make my learners bicultural. I never tried to make my English learners French, into French children with two identities. My answer is I want my learners to acquire a new competence, not a new identity. And they should be able to mediate, to see themselves as others see them.

Intercultural Competence and Mediation

Mediation is an interesting word. Teachers are mediators. For example, think about your history teachers and what they did for you, a learner, when you were at school or university. They tried to give you a sense of what it was like living in China, or anywhere else, at a different period of time. The best history teachers try to put their learners into a different time, and to experience for a moment what it is like to be in a different time. Not to change their identity, but to see the world from a different time perspective.

The same thing should happen in language teaching, in the sense that teachers of Chinese will help their learners to understand Chinese culture, the ways of doing things in China as well as reflect upon on their own way. That is one aspect of mediation. Let us look a little more at this idea of mediation in the following simple drawing:

On the left hand side is a Chinese person who might be a teacher, a mother, a father, who knows, many different identities. On the right hand side, is let's say an American person, who may be a teacher, a mother, a father, a footballer, all kinds of identities. Each of these has in their heads the cultures which they have acquired by becoming a Chinese, a teacher, a mother, etc. – each of their identities which make them members of social groups. People learn their culture of being a Chinese mainly at school. They learn the culture of being a teacher when they are trained on a teacher training course. The same applies to the person on the right hand side.

In the middle is the successful learner,

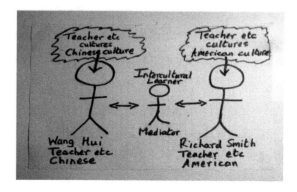

Mediator for Others

的很多老师在教学过程中都遇到过问题，因为学生对中国老师的教学有着不同的理解。这时中国老师就需要一个中介，在中国人和美国人之间进行调和，通常是一个像丽虹这样的人，她了解两种文化，因而可以作为中介向中国老师解释美国的学生期待怎样的课堂体验，同时也可以向美国学生解释中国老师期望怎样的课堂效果。为了达到这一目的，她时而说汉语时而说英语，以便向一方说明另一方的想法。在这个过程中，她就是处在第三空间的。

现在我们再来谈论另一种中介。一个优秀的跨文化学习者应该能够充当自己的中介。这是一种全新的第三空间。在之前举的例子中，我们谈到的是实在的空间，是一个人站在两种文化之间，扮演着中介的角色。但这个全新的第三空间是虚拟的空间，学习者自身就是中介。

Mediator for myself

在这张图中，右手边是"他者"，假设他是一个中国人。学习者位于左侧，由于学习了汉语，他能够跳出自身的文化框架，进入一个虚拟的空间，在这里，他可以向自己阐释他所探索到的中国文化，并将其与母文化进行对比和比较。从这个意义上说，学习者自身就是中介，但他是在为自己做调和的工作。他们开始以他者的目光来审视自身，使所有熟悉的内容（即他们在自己文化中所积累的经验）变得陌生化，同时使陌生的东西（即通过学习一门外语——比如汉语——所获得的知识和经验）变得熟悉。

在前几次讲座中我们提到的关于圣诞节的例子里，学生要把圣诞节在英国和保加利亚这两个国家里的不同含义解释给其他的保加利亚学生。而在西班牙语的例子中，学生要学会把一个国家的水果文化解释给另一个国家的人。

someone who knows how to mediate between the two, who can explain one to the other. Let us take the example of teacher culture. The mediator can explain to Richard Smith the culture of teaching that Wang Hui has in his head. The mediator is able to take a middle position and explain: 'In China, the beliefs about teaching are X, Y and Z. In America, the beliefs of teaching are A, B and C.' In order for Richard Smith to understand the Chinese way of thinking about teaching, he needs to see the similarity and difference between A and X, between beliefs in America about teaching and beliefs in China about teaching. The mediator takes up a 'third space' between the two people, a space which is neither Chinese nor American.

As a real-life example, Lihong said that her experience in the US is that teachers in the Confucius Institute may have some problems because the students have different understandings of teaching from the Chinese teachers. The Chinese teachers need a mediator. And usually that is someone like Lihong who has an understanding of both and acts as a mediator to explain to the Chinese teachers what the American students expect in the classroom and to the American students what the Chinese teacher expects to do in the classroom. In order to do this, she speaks sometimes Chinese sometimes English to explain to each side what the other expects. In doing so she takes up a position in the third space.

We can now go to another kind of mediation. We can think of a good intercultural learner as someone who can mediate for themselves. This is a different kind of third space. In the previous one, it's a literal space. It is somebody standing between two others and acting as a mediator. In this second case, it's a virtual third space. The mediator is the learner himself or herself.

Here on the right hand side is 'the other'; let's suppose it's a Chinese person. The learner on the left, as a consequence of being taught Chinese, is able to stand outside of him/herself in a virtual space, and see and explain to themselves what it is that they are discovering about Chinese culture, and compare and contrast it with their own. In that sense the learner is a mediator, but he or she is mediating for themselves. They are beginning to see themselves as others to see them. They are beginning to make strange that which is familiar – what they know already from their experience of their own cultures – and to make familiar that which is strange, that which they are learning about and experiencing through learning a foreign language – in this case Chinese.

What we saw in the examples I have given in earlier lectures is that the learners were learning to explain the concept of Christmas in Britain and in Bulgaria to other Bulgarians. In the Spanish classroom example, they were learning to explain fruit eating in one country to people in another. In the chopsticks

在关于筷子的例子里，学习中国语言文化的美国人要学会向其他美国人解释筷子及其相关的一切。就做自己的中介而言，他们正学着掌握一些新的知识，并将自己头脑中已有的知识与这些新知识进行对比和比较。

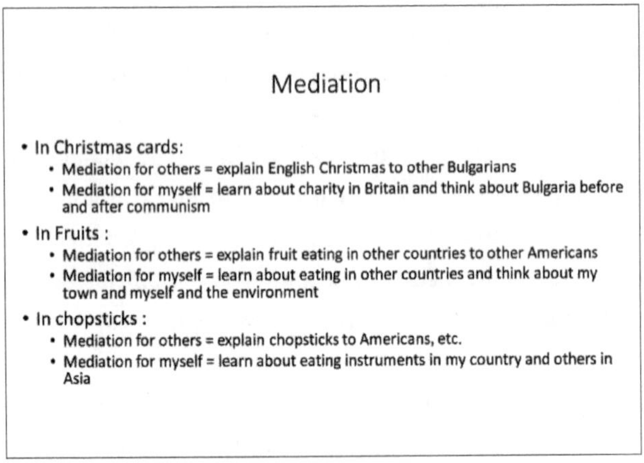
Mediation
• In Christmas cards:
• Mediation for others = explain English Christmas to other Bulgarians
• Mediation for myself = learn about charity in Britain and think about Bulgaria before and after communism
• In Fruits :
• Mediation for others = explain fruit eating in other countries to other Americans
• Mediation for myself = learn about eating in other countries and think about my town and myself and the environment
• In chopsticks :
• Mediation for others = explain chopsticks to Americans, etc.
• Mediation for myself = learn about eating instruments in my country and others in Asia

“批判性思维”和“在社区中行动”

跨文化交际能力与“批判性思维”

在这一部分我想谈论两个概念 ：“批判性思维”或“批判性”，以及“在社区中行动”。

到目前为止我们谈到的比较和批判性分析的问题，即批判地分析其他文化中的人如何行为处事，并将其与自身文化进行对比，这就是我所说的批判性文化意识，涉及分析和判断两个方面。拿保加利亚的例子来说，学生起初以非常简单的概念展开讨论，比如圣诞贺卡，到最后他们不仅是分析圣诞贺卡本身，还要分析更为深层次的文化内涵，比如在英国你买圣诞贺卡的时候，实际上有一部分钱捐给了慈善机构，从而可以帮助非洲人民。然后他们把这种情况与过去的保加利亚进行比较，发现保加利亚的情形完全不同。他们还比较了英国那些帮助穷人的慈善机构和保加利亚政府的不同，发现在英国，穷人得到的帮助并不来自政府。

这就意味着他们开始对他们自己的社会和英国社会做出判断。他们分析人们的行为，并考虑这些行为背后的价值理念。如果人们买圣诞贺卡并捐钱给慈善机构，这就表明在英国社会中存在某些价值理念，在当时的保加利亚

example, American learners of Chinese languaculture were learning to explain chopsticks and everything connected with chopsticks to other Americans. In terms of mediating for themselves, they were learning something new and comparing and contrasting what they have in their heads with what is present in other cultures.

'Critical Thinking' and 'Action in the Community'

Intercultural competence and critical thinking

In this section I want to talk about two concepts: 'critical thinking' or 'criticality' and, second, 'action in the community'.

Everything that I have said so far about comparison and about critically analysing what people do in other cultures and compare it with one's own, is what I mean by critical cultural awareness. It's a matter of analysing and making judgments. In the Bulgarian example, the students start with something simple like a Christmas card, and eventually they were analysing not only Christmas cards but the idea that in England when you buy a Christmas card, you contribute a small amount of money to charity and that money helps people in Africa, for example. They were comparing that with what happened in Bulgaria in the past. It was nothing like that in Bulgaria. They were also comparing charities in Britain which help poor people, comparing the fact that in Bulgaria, there are poor people who need help which they don't get from government, with their own government.

This means that they were beginning to make judgments about what is happening in their own society and in British society. They were analysing what people do and they were thinking about the values behind what people do. If people buy a Christmas card and give some money to the charity, then there are certain values there which are present in British society, and which were, at the time, not present in Bulgarian society. They made judgments about those values, beliefs and behaviours that people

---

Critical thinking / Critical cultural awareness

• **Analysis** and **'judgement'**

• **Analyse** what people 'do' and 'values and beliefs' for why they do what they do [EXAMPLE: send Christmas cards]

• **Judge** values, beliefs and behaviours [EXAMPLE: 'charity' ; 'communism']
  o By what criteria? Is the learner conscious of criteria used?
  o Role of teacher – tell learners what to think? Allow learners to judge? Make learners explain judgement?
  o = teacher's dilemma

社会中是没有的。他们会对人们在社会中所体现出的这些价值观、理念和行为进行评判。

问题是：这种判断的标准是什么？如果说学生考虑的是保加利亚和英国的穷人，他们需要帮助却无法获得政府的援助，那么这些学生就要思考，出现这样的境况究竟对不对？如果说穷人需要帮助，那么判断依据又是什么？有些人认为穷人就是需要帮助，这是非常明显的事实，但是有些人并不认同这一事实，觉得穷人应该对自己的命运负责。如果学生觉得答案显而易见，他们就要问问自己为什么这么想。

在这种情况下，老师的角色并不是告诉学生怎么想——帮助穷人是对是错——而是应该让学生学会做出判断，学会思考为什么他们要做出自己的判断。这是老师困境的另一个方面。老师的职责不是去告诉学生怎么思考，而是帮助学生建立起批判性思维，独立思考。以上就是我提出两个概念中的第一个：批判性／批判性思维／批判的文化意识。

跨文化交际能力与"在社区中行动"

现在我们来看第二个概念：在社区中行动。我会通过两个例子来解释这一概念。

第一个例子是一个项目，在这个案例中，话题是由老师和学生们共同选定的，是自由选择的结果。在之前我们看到的例子中，都是话题选择了老师，老师只能根据给定的话题进行项目设计。这个项目在一所英国的大学和一所阿根廷的大学同时展开，两所大学的老师都可以自己选择教学的内容和话题。

这个案例里的语言学习者都是高阶水平的，教学内容都来自2012年的时事，而我给大家的介绍来源于参与这个项目的老师们所撰写的描述。2012年，英阿战争结束30周年。这场战争的起因是一起岛屿纠纷，英国称之为福克兰群岛，阿根廷称之为马尔维纳斯群岛（简称"马岛"）。为了纪念战争结束30周年，英阿媒体都在报道这一事件。当时有两位老师，一位在阿根廷的大学里面教英语，另一位在英国的大学里教西班牙语，他们通过网络进行合作，而他们的合作只是一个更大项目中的一部分。这个项目是鼓励老师结成两人或三人合作小组，通过网络进行合作。其大致内容是这样的：

have in the society.

The question is: What are their criteria? If they are thinking about the poor people in their society, the poor people in Bulgaria, and the poor people in Britain who need help but don't get it from their government, they need to ask themselves whether this is right or wrong and what their criteria for saying that poor people should be helped are. It might seem obvious that the poor should be helped, but some people would say it's not obvious and that poor people must take responsibility for their own fates. If learners think the answer is obvious, they need to ask themselves why they think it's obvious.

In this situation, the role of the teacher is not to tell the learners what to think – that it's good or bad to help poor people – but rather to help them to learn to make judgments, to learn to think about why they are making judgments. That is another aspect of the teacher's dilemma. It's not the teachers' job to tell the learners what to think. The teachers' job is to help the learners to be critical and to think for themselves. That is the first of my two concepts: criticality/critical thinking/critical cultural awareness.

Intercultural competence and 'action in the community'

I turn now to the second concept: action in the community. I will do this by giving two examples.

The first is a project, and in this case, the topic was chosen by the teachers and the students; it was a free choice. In other cases as we have seen, teachers are given a topic, and have to make the project out of what they are given. This project takes place in a British university and in an Argentinean university, where the teachers can decide their own topics.

This example is with advanced learners of language. The topic came from contemporary events in 2012, and my explanation is based on a description written by the teachers involved. 2012 was the 30th anniversary of a war between Britain and Argentina, a war about what in Britain are called the Falkland Islands, and in Argentina are called the Malvinas. Because it was the 30th anniversary,

Falklands/Malvinas Project

Citizenship education for a culture of peace: The case of the Malvinas/Falklands project in language teaching in Higher Education
Melina Porto & Leticia Yulita

In: Byram, Golubeva, Han and Wagner (eds) (1st Nov 2016) Education for Intercultural Citizenship – Principles in Practice. Multilingual Matters

The Malvinas/Falklands War (1982): An opportunity for citizenship education in the foreign language classroom in Argentina and the UK

50 Argentinean university students of English (CEFR C1) AND 50 UK students of Spanish (Honours)
AIMS – THINKING
* encouraging STUDENTS to explore and reflect on historical issues – nationally and internationally
* understand historical issues and how to analyse them in national and international context,
* challenge taken-for-granted assumptions about history
AIMS – ACTING
* Research (historical documents – newspapers, interviews...)
* Communicate with people about historical issues – from international perspective

researched conflict and – focus on interaction based on respect, mutual understanding and cooperative conflict resolution

一共有两组学生：一组是在阿根廷学习英语的学生，另一组是在英国一所大学学习西班牙语的学生。老师和学生都通过互联网展开合作。

在这个过程中老师的目标是什么？首先，正如孔子所言，要让学生去思考。老师要让学生去**探索和反思**一个历史事件，一场 30 年前发生的战争。他要让学生从**国家和国际**的角度去看待历史，希望学生不仅以**国家思维思考**，也能以**国际思维思考**。他们希望学生能够从国家和国际两个视角**理解**、**分析**历史问题。换句话说，老师希望学生掌握我之前提到的那些技能：学会如何探索、对比、阐释和批判性地分析。因此，这也挑战了学生对历史事件的既有观点，并对这些观点进行批判性地分析和思考。老师还要让学生进行**研究**，运用探索的能力去历史文件中习得更多关于这场战争的信息，然后让学生同另一个国家和文化的人交流自己运用国际视角所发现的信息，并在这个过程中合作以解决冲突。老师也希望学生能"在社区中行动"。简而言之，老师要把语言文化教学、跨文化能力和公民教育的某些方面结合在一起。

他们实际上都做了哪些工作？首先在第一个阶段，每一组学生分别在课上和课外做一些研究，研究 30 年前那场战争以及媒体对此的报道。他们读了 30 年以前的报纸，因为这些大学生只有 20 多岁，战争爆发的时候他们还没有出生，所以这些对他们来说就是历史。因此从某种意义上说，他们不光是为自己和他人做文化调和，同时也在调和不同的历史视角。比如，在阿根廷，学生们读旧报纸是他们的作业，然后为远在大西洋彼岸的英国小组成员们准备一个英语的介绍；同样地，英国学生要根据他们读到的内容准备一个西班牙语的介绍，然后他们在网上进行小组交流。因为班级很大，老师要把

it was in the newspapers, both in Argentina and in Britain. The two teachers, one working in Argentina teaching English as a foreign language, and one working in England teaching Spanish as a foreign language, work together through the Internet, and this particular project is part of a network of projects, where teachers work together in pairs or in threes through the Internet. Here is an overview:

There are two groups of learners: one group in Argentina learning English, one group of learners at university in England learning Spanish. The two teachers use the Internet for cooperation as do the learners.

What are the teachers' aims here? First of all, as Confucius said, we want our learners to think. The teachers want their students to *explore and reflect* on a historical topic, the war 30 years before. They want them to do that from a *national perspective* but also in an *international* perspective. They want them to think internationally not just nationally. They want them to *understand* the historical issues, and be able to *analyse* those issues in both national and international perspectives. In other words, the teachers want their students to learn the same competences as I have discussed earlier: knowing how to discover, how to compare and contrast, how to interpret, and how to critically analyse. They want therefore to challenge them to take the assumptions that they have about their history and to think analytically and critically about those assumptions. They want them to carry out *research*, use the competences of discovery to learn more about the war from historical documents. They want them to be able to communicate what they have discovered from an international perspective, and to interact with people from another country and culture, and be able to cooperate about the conflict. They also want them to take 'action in the community'. In short, they are going to combine teaching of languaculture, intercultural competence with some aspects of citizenship education.

What do they actually do in practice? The first stage is that each group separately, in their own classroom and in their own time outside the classroom, does some research about what happened 30 years before, and how the events were presented in the media. They read the newspapers from 30 years before and since they are students in the university who are only 20 years or so old, not even born when the events took place, this is for them history. In a sense therefore, they are not just mediating their own culture perspective for others and themselves but they are also mediating historical perspectives. For example, in Argentina, they read the old newspapers – as homework – and then they prepare an explanation in English for the English group on the other side of the Atlantic. And vice versa, the English group prepare an explanation of what they have read in Spanish.

他们分成小组，也许六人一组，然后从阿根廷的视角和英国的视角分别发言并将 30 年前的这两种视角进行对比和比较。

他们也做了一些其他的事情。有的学生成功采访了一两位 30 年前参战的老兵，他们都已经 50 多岁了。有意思的是，通过互联网，在英国学习西班牙语的英国学生就可以同步听到阿根廷学生对阿根廷老兵做的西班牙语采访了，而且他们也可以向老兵提问。这是学生们做过的最有冒险性、最有野心的一件事了。当然其他学生也做了其他有趣的事，并且把他们的项目报告放到了 Facebook 或博客这样的社交网络上。

进行对比和比较，不是为了得出一方视角优于另一方这样的结论，而是要从第三方视角，即国际视角、跨大西洋的视角来看待历史事件。

Activities

STAGE 1 – DISCOVER ABOUT 'US' AND PREPARE FOR 'THEM'

- researched newspapers, talked with parents, created PPTs about the war

STAGE 2 – PRESENT 'US' TO 'THEM' AND COMPARE

- communicated synchronically and diachronically (wiki and Elluminate)
- interviewed Argentine and English war veteran
  - created blogs/facebook pages and noting reactions

STAGE 3 – WORK TOGETHER – IN 'US AND THEM' GROUP

- collaboratively created leaflets, etc. to show both national perspectives and reconciliation

---

在第三阶段，两国学生的小组进行合作，通过 Skype、邮件等方式来沟通。他们要共同合作展示 30 年前双方对这场战争的观点。他们从第三空间，也就是中介的角度来看待问题，或者用他们自己的话来说，是要中和两种相反的视角。这是他们的研究成果，一份记录了"一个事件的两面"的文件：

这是 30 年前英阿两国媒体报道的集合，可以看出双方都有极端的民族主义倾向。学生用英西两种语言分别做了评论，最后总结说："要独立思考"，"没人能左右你的思想"，每个人都应该"看到事情的两面"。他们利用这份共同创作出的文件阐释了新视角。在另一份文件中，内容都由西班牙语写成，但仍然兼顾了两种观点。

Then they talk to each other using the Internet, in small groups. Since the classes are quite large, the teachers put them into smaller groups, maybe six people in each group, and they present to each other the Argentinean perspective on the war, and then the British perspective. They compare and contrast these two perspectives from 30 years ago.

They also did other things. Some of them managed to find and interview one or two men who had been soldiers in the war 30 years before, men in their 50s. The interesting thing is that with the Internet you can have Argentinean students speaking to an Argentinean soldier in Spanish and be listened to by an English learner of Spanish in England. And that English learner of Spanish can also interview the soldier. That was one of the most adventurous, ambitious things they did. But other students also did other interesting things and put reports of their project on Facebook or blogs and so on.

So now they have compared and contrasted, not to say one perspective is better than the other, but to see it from a third position, third place, an international perspective, a trans-Atlantic perspective.

The third stage is that in their groups, they work together and they talk to each other by Skype and emails and so on, in mixed groups of Argentinean and English students. They work together to create something which will show both sides of the events 30 years 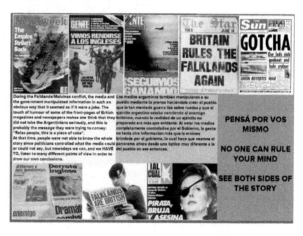 earlier. They look from a third space perspective, a mediating perspective, or to use their words, a reconciliation of two opposing perspectives. Here is one document they produced to show 'Both sides of the story':

It is a mixture of British and Argentinean newspapers from 30 years ago, where both were very extremely nationalistic. The students also comment, in English and in Spanish, summarising their views as 'Think for yourself', 'No one can rule your mind', and one should 'See both sides of the story'. They use this documentary which they produce together as a means of giving a new perspective. In the next document, everything is in Spanish, but it still gives two perspectives.

　　之所以用西班牙语写，是因为他们要把这些传单发到街上，在街头采取行动。我们看到一个学生正在发传单并和路人讲话，试图将他们与英国学生的合作项目向路人解释清楚，而马岛战争在阿根廷媒体中是非常敏感的热议话题。

　　总之，学生们是"在社区中行动"，这个概念出自公民教育领域。在欧洲的公民教育中，或某种程度上美国的公民教育中，老师不只是传授关于国家政治制度的相关知识，而是鼓励学生在自己所在的社区里（可大可小）采取行动。在这种情况下，他们的行动受到了大西洋彼岸学生的影响，他们一起合作交流，因而在看待牵扯到两国的历史事件时获得了一种国际的、跨文化的视野。

　　"在社区中行动"其实有很多不同的类型。有些学生是发传单，有些则是去当地的学校教书，并在教学过程中使用他们共同开发出的教材。有些则是把所获得的信息上传到 YouTube 等网站上。

'Action in the Community'

STAGE 4

- Distributed leaflets
- Taught special class in English language school
- Taught class with NGO in poor neighbourhood [youtube]
- ETC.

It is in Spanish because they are going to distribute their leaflets in the street and they are going to take action in the street. In the next slide we see a student who is distributing a leaflet in the street and talking to people, trying to explain to them the work that they've been doing with English students about something which was very topical and sensitive issue in newspaper in Argentina.

• Melina Porto (2014): Intercultural citizenship education in an EFL online project in Argentina, Language and Intercultural Communication, DOI:10.1080/14708477.2014.890625
• Melina Porto and Michael Byram (2015) A curriculum for action in the community and intercultural citizenship in higher education. *Language Culture and Curriculum* 28, 3, 226-242.

In short, the students were taking 'action in the community', a concept which is taken from citizenship education. In citizenship education in Europe, and to some extent in the US, teachers don't just teach the political system of their country. They encourage their learners to take action now in their own community, large or small. In this case, that action has been influenced by the fact that the students work together interacting with the students on the other side of the Atlantic and gain an international, intercultural perspective on historical events which their two countries were involved in.

The 'actions in the community' were of different kinds. Some students distributed leaflets. Some went to teach in their local schools where they used the materials which they had produced together. And some of them put things on YouTube and so on.

The second example is from a secondary school. The same approach takes place here. The learners interact by the Internet and they do something in their own environment. In this case, the topic is about the environment, 'being green' and doing something for your environment.

我要举的第二个例子是中学生的例子。在这里用的也是同样的方法。学生们通过互联网交流，然后在自己所处的环境中采取行动。这个案例中的话题是关于环保的："维护绿色"，为你的环境做点儿什么。

Green Kidz project

Green Kidz: Young learners engage in intercultural environmental citizenship in English language classroom in Argentina and Denmark.

Melina Porto, Petra Daryai-Hansen, María Emilia Arcuri and Kira Schifler

In: Byram, Golubeva, Han and Wagner (eds) 2016, Education for Intercultural Citizenship – Principles in Practice. Multilingual Matters

项目执行的过程也是类似的。通过同样的社区行动来对阿根廷和丹麦的环保问题进行对比和比较。

"在社区中行动"包括制作视频，登上当地的报纸，在街上拉起横幅，在社区中宣传他们在学校所做的事情。

在这两个例子中，学生们都变得具有批判性了。他们都会分析人们在战争中或在环保方面采取的行动。他们通过这一被我称为"自由社会"（liberal society）的清晰且基础的标准来评判他人的行为。他们在社区里采取了行动，但是因为他们建立了国际联系，和其他国家的人讨论了这个话题，从另一个

The stages of the project are similar. There is the comparison and contrast between Argentina and Denmark, the same kind of action in the community.

As 'actions in the community', the students created videos, got themselves into the local newspaper, put a banner in the street to advertise what they were doing in the school, to bring into the community the work that they were doing in the school.

In both examples, the learners are becoming critical. They are analysing what people do, in war time or in the environment. They are judging what people do on the basis of a clear underlying idea, that I will call the idea of liberavl society. They are taking action in their community but it is different from what they might have done without their international

---

Participants and aims

Learners in Argentina and in Denmark – learning English (ages 10-12) – connected by Internet

Aims:

THINKING
- encourage children to explore and reflect on environmental issues - globally and locally,
- understand environmental issues and how to recognise them in their own surroundings,
- challenge taken-for-granted representations of the environment

ACTING
- engage in trash sorting and recycling practices,
- contribute to improving the environment in their local communities = ACTION IN THE COMMUNITY

Activities

STAGE 1 – DISCOVER ABOUT 'US' AND PREPARE FOR 'THEM'
- pupils identified green crimes in their schools and in their communities and drew or video-taped these crimes,
- trash analysis listing, classifying and sorting trash in waste bins in schools

STAGE 2 – PRESENT 'US' TO 'THEM' AND COMPARE
- compared and discussed results using a wiki,
- survey among family members, friends, etc. about their environmental habits - compared on wiki,
- analysed critically (audio) visual media images and texts, produced in Argentina and in Denmark

STAGE 3 – WORK TOGETHER – IN 'US AND THEM' GROUP
- collaboratively online using skype and wiki (ie Argentinean and Danish pupils in mixed groups) designed advertisements to raise awareness of environmental issues

---

Action in the community

STAGE 4 – FOCUS AGAIN ON 'US' AND ACTING...

Argentine pupils:
- created videos and songs and shared in facebook page,
- were interviewed by a local journalist and got the collaborative posters published in local newspaper,
- designed a banner and hung in the school street.

---

connections, where they discussed the topic with people in another country, from another perspective. They have acquired an international intercultural perspective. They are being mediators between 'them and us'. The teacher has encouraged them to take action. So in this case the teachers have thought about the teacher's

角度去思考，所以他们所采取的行动会因此而不同，他们已经具备了国际性的跨文化视角。他们在"他们和我们"之间充当中介，在老师的鼓励下采取行动。所以在这个案例中，老师们考虑到了自身的困境，并认为老师有责任鼓励学生走进社区采取行动，公民教育课的老师可能也会这么做。并不是所有的老师都会这么做，但是这些老师决定这么做，而这正是教师困境中的一部分。

The meaning of the examples

- Learners are critical
- → analyse what people do [in war; in environment]
- → judge what they do according to criteria of liberal societies

- Learners take action [after discussing with international partners; in their own community]
- → act as mediators between perspectives ['theirs' and 'ours']
- → teachers encourage action – teacher's dilemma.

社会中的语言教学——以欧洲为例

在最后这部分我要强调的是，语言教学、语言文化教学以及跨文化能力教学——这些都是我刚才谈到的活动的不同叫法——和"社会责任"是密切相关的。在欧洲人们是这么去看的，至于在中国是不是这样就得由大家来决定了。

欧洲存在一些众所周知的严峻社会问题。一年多以前在法国发生了"《查理周刊》惨案"，而自那以后，还发生过其他恐怖袭击活动。这些都是社会痼疾，我们已经心知肚明。早在2008年，欧洲委员会就在思考如何通过教育塑造一个跨文化的社会。这就意味着跨文化语言教学已经成为塑造更开放的思维方式的一小块组成部分。

这些组织希望通过教育推动改变，使欧洲人具备更多跨文化的意识，他们希望通过"民主的公民教育"和"跨文化的对话"来实现这个目标。

作为这个活动的一分子，我们一直想建立一个跨文化交际能力的模型，不仅适用于外语教学，也适用于学校里的所有学科。这其中也包括大学，但是重点要放在其他层次的学校上，因为每个人都得上学，但不是每个人都能

dilemma, and they have decided that it is part of the teacher's job to encourage the learners to go out into the community and take action, as citizenship teachers might also do. Not everybody would do that, but these teachers have decided for themselves, and again this is part of the teacher's dilemma.

Language Teaching in Society – the European Example

In the next and final part, I want to emphasise that language teaching/languaculture teaching/intercultural competence teaching – different terms for the activities I have been describing – is related to the concept of 'social responsibility'. This is a European perspective and whether it is appropriate in China is for you to deicide.

As is well known there are major social problems in Europe. More than a year ago, there was a massacre in France at a magazine called *Charlie Hebdo*, and since then, there has been other terrorist activities. We have known about these problems for a long

> Language Teaching in Society
> – the European Example
>
> • The European situation – 'Charlie-Hebdo' and after
> • Before 'Charlie-Hebdo' – 2008 'European Year of Intercultural Dialogue and White (Policy) Paper on 'Living together... Intercultural Dialogue'
>
> • Education as a means to create change
>   • Education for citizenship
>   • Education for democratic citizenship [and intercultural dialogue]
>   → Model of Competences for Democratic Culture [and intercultural dialogue]
>   → how to plan ALL subjects to develop Competences...
>   http://www.coe.int/t/dg4/education/competences_en.asp

time. Already in 2008, the Council of Europe were thinking about how we can create a more intercultural society through education. This means that intercultural teaching is a small part of a wider way of thinking.

These organisations want to create change through education, to make us Europeans more intercultural, and they want to do this through 'education for democratic citizenship' and 'intercultural dialogue'.

As part of this activity, we have been thinking about how we can produce a model of intercultural competence which can be used not just in foreign language teaching but in all subjects at school. Also in universities but the focus is upon school because everybody has to go to school, whereas only some people go to university.

The model that I have used so far in these lectures which was first presented in the book that I wrote in 1997, is a model for language teaching. A model for all

够上大学。

我在这几次讲座中使用的模型最早出现在我 1997 年写的那本书里，是用于语言教学的。而一个适用于所有学科的模型肯定还会复杂得多。

下面的"蝴蝶模型"是为民主文化的能力（CDC）（欧洲委员会，2016）设计的模型，左侧列出了所有价值观和技巧方面的内容，是"怎么做的知识"，右上角是态度方面的内容，右下角则是关于"是什么的知识"。所以如果一个良好的欧洲公民想成为具有跨文化能力的公民，他或她就需要具备价值观、技能、态度、知识和批判性的理解能力。

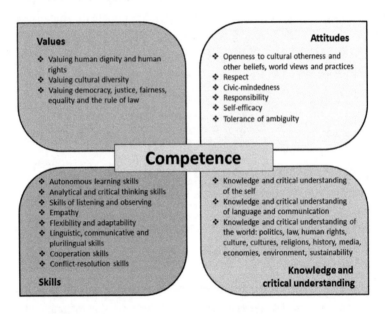

这些都是非常抽象的概念。现在让我们从蝴蝶每一片翅膀上的第一个能力说起。价值观：尊重人类的尊严和权利。如果你想成为一名优秀的跨文化公民，这一价值观是必备的。态度：对他者及他者的信仰、价值观和行为保持开放的态度。如果你想成为一名优秀的跨文化公民，这是你必备的态度之一。左下角是技能：要有自主学习技能。要具备自学的能力，为自己而学，这也是我在给大家举例的时候一直强调的一点。右下角是知识和对自我的批判性认知：了解你自己，了解语言与交际，了解社会。这些都是能力。

这个模型描述了跨文化交际能力的各种价值观。学生们在社区中采取行动的种种例子就是他们在利用自己的能力改善社会。

subjects is going to be much more complex.

The 'butterfly model' of Competences for Democratic Culture (CDC) (Council of Europe, 2016) below lists values and skills, 'knowing how', on the left hand side, attitudes on the top right hand side, and the 'knowledge that' on the bottom right hand side. These are the values, skills, attitudes and knowledge and critical understanding that a good European citizen needs if he or she is going to be an interculturally competent citizen.

These are very abstract ideas. So let's just take the first competence on each wing. Values: Valuing human dignity and human rights. If you are going to be a good intercultural citizen, then that must be one of your values. Attitudes: Openness to otherness and other beliefs, values and practices. If you are going to be a good intercultural citizen, that's one of the attitudes you must have. Skills on the left hand side: Autonomous learning skills. You must have the knowledge how to do things for yourself, to learn for yourself. That's one of the things I have been emphasising in my examples. On the right hand side: knowledge and critical understanding of the self. Knowing about yourself, about language and communication, about society. These are the competences.

> **Malvinas/Falklands and Green Kidz**
>
> • Existed before CDC
> • Demonstrate CDC competences FOR EXAMPLE:
> **Valuing democracy, justice, fairness, equality and the rule of law**
> • This set of values is based on the general belief that societies ought to operate and be governed through democratic processes which respect the principles of justice, fairness, equality and the rule of law.

> **Malvinas/Falklands and Green Kidz**
>
> • **Openness to cultural otherness and to other beliefs, world views and practices**
> • Openness is an attitude towards people (...) or towards beliefs, world views and practices which differ from one's own. It involves (...) willingness to engage with other people and other perspectives on the world.
> **Responsibility**
> • Responsibility (...) involves being reflective about one's actions, (...) about how to act in a morally appropriate way, (...) performing those actions and holding oneself accountable for the outcomes of those actions.

The model is a statement the values of intercultural competence. In all of the examples where the students take action in the community, they use their competences to try to improve their society.

In fact, the approach of languaculture/intercultural language teaching is the approach the Council of Europe is now taking. For example, in the example focused on the Falklands/Malvinas, we can find one of the values of the butterfly model—valuing

事实上，语言文化／跨文化语言教学的方法就是现在欧洲委员会在使用的方法。比如在前面提到的马岛的例子中，我们可以找到蝴蝶模型中提到的一些价值观，如珍视民主、正义、公正、平等和法制。模型中的其他维度都列在了下面，在我给出的教学案例中也都能找到，在这里我就不赘述了。

Malvinas/Falklands and Green Kidz

- **Linguistic, communicative and plurilingual skills**
- (...) the skills required to communicate (...) with people who speaks the same or another language, and to act as a mediator between speakers of different languages.
- **Knowledge and critical understanding of language and communication**
- (...) of the socially appropriate verbal and non-verbal communicative conventions that operate in the language(s) which one speaks, (...) of how every language expresses culturally shared meanings in a unique way.

作为一名语言文化教师，我认为这些就是我们现在该做的事情。作为语言文化教师，我们应以教育为工具，提升和改造我们的社会。但是正如我之前说过的，作为教师这是一个我们不得不思考的困境。每个人都应该独立思考这一问题。我无法告诉大家该思考些什么，老师有责任做出自己的判断。

这就是我的结论。

谢谢大家。

*　　　　　*　　　　　*

☺ 交流互动

提问人 1：非常感谢。我的问题是关于跨文化交际的教学法。我现在就在教跨文化交际。在教授"是什么的知识"和"怎么做

democracy, justice, fairness, equality and the rule of law. Other aspects of the CDC model are listed in the slides below and can be found in the examples of teaching I have given, but I will not labour the point here as we reach the end of the lecture.

My belief as a languaculture teacher is that this is what we should be doing. As languaculture teachers, we should be part of how education improves and changes society.

And...

• 'action in the community' = using competences in life (in education, and in society)

• Language teaching can/should influence and change society
    • The teacher's dilemma – Shall I teach my learners to take ;action in the community'

Conclusion

• Teachers have responsibility – have dilemmas – must take own decisions

But as I said before, this is a dilemma which we all have to consider as teachers for ourselves. Everyone has to think for themselves. It is not for me to tell other teachers what to think. Teachers have their responsibilities and must make their own decisions.

That's my conclusion.

Thank you.

*   *   *

☺ Interaction and Communication

Questioner 1: Thank you Mike. My question is about the teaching methodology of intercultural communication. I'm teaching intercultural communication right now. What is the proportion you mentioned of teaching 'knowing that' to 'knowing how'? Is there any proportion between them? Or is there any order? Should we teach 'knowing how' first or second?

Michael Byram: I would say that if you list your objectives for your teaching,

的知识"时，其比例是怎样的？两者孰轻孰重？或者是否存在一个教学顺序的问题。我们是否应该先教"怎么做的知识"，再教"是什么的知识"？

Michael Byram：如果你把你的教学目标列出来，比如，"这门课结束后，我的学生将知道……他们还要学会……"，那么"怎么做的知识"就要比"是什么的知识"更重要。至于时间分配，在我刚给出的例子中，学生们在学习"怎么做的知识"上的确花了更多的时间，我想这样做是合适的。当然，我们也必须要教一些"是什么的知识"，老师也可以帮助学生来理解这些知识。但是从长远来看，"怎么做的知识"要比"是什么的知识"更有用处。人们常说"授之以鱼，不如授之以渔"，说的其实就是这个道理。所以我想应多学"怎么做的知识"。但这两者是相互联系的，因为通过将"怎么做的知识"付诸实践，你也会获得"是什么的知识"。

提问人 2：您刚才谈到教师的困境。我觉得教师在外语教学中应该保持中立，但几年前当我开始学习英语时，我听说如果学生置身于外国文化中，他们学习交际能力和外语的速度可能会更快。您是不是认同这种观点？

Michael Byram：有一种叫做"融合性动机"的理论支持了这一说法。另外一派理论认为，如果我们可以利用实际的内容进行教学，并且在认知过程中讨论这些内容、理智地参与这

些内容，做些激励学生的活动，那么语言能力就能够得到同步提高。但这不意味着你一定要认同这种文化，你当然可以暂时以对方的视角看问题，但并不是说要完全采取他者的视角。至少我不认为应该这样做。我不认为认同了其他文化，你的外语就会学得更好。

and you say 'by the end of my lessons, students will know that…, and they will know how…', then 'knowing how' is more important than 'knowing that'. In terms of time, in the examples that I have given you, the learners spent more time improving 'knowing how' than they did in acquiring 'knowledge that'. I think that's appropriate. Of course there's got to be some 'knowing that', and of course the teacher can help them to 'know that'. But in a longer term, the 'knowing how' is more productive than 'knowing that'. Somebody once said, give a man or a woman a fish, then they eat for a day; give them a rod to fish, and they eat for a lifetime. It's the same kind of idea. I would say more 'knowing how' than 'knowing that'. But things are always inter-connected, because by practicing your skills of 'knowing how', you acquire 'knowing that'.

Questioner 2: I was listening to your speech about the teacher's dilemma. I think a teacher should keep neutral in teaching a foreign language. But when I started learning English several years ago, I heard that if the students try to put themselves into the foreign culture, they might acquire the communicative skills and the language a little bit faster. Do you believe in that?

Michael Byram: There is the literature on 'integrative motivation' which would suggest that. Another body of research says that by using content, talking about content, engaging with content intellectually and doing something which is stimulating, then language competence improves at the same time. But it does not necessarily mean that you identify with the other. You can of course temporarily see the other as others see us. But it's not a matter of taking a totally different view. That would not be my view of what we need to do. I don't think identifying with another culture will make you a better language learner.

Questioner 3: Thank you Mike. Your speech is very impressive. My question might be a little difficult. As I know, you established your ICC model in 1997 about 20 years past. Now your theory not only concerns language but also has something to do with citizenship education. So I want to know your opinion about your theory. Could you comment on your theory yourself?

Michael Byram: The addition of the dimension of citizenship education is something which became clear to me after my book written in 1997. During the 2000s with my colleagues in the university, we had lots of seminars and we published books about citizenship education. My idea was to try to combine that

提问人 3：谢谢，您的讲座令我受益匪浅。我的问题可能有点难。就我所知，您早在 1997 年就提出了 ICC 模型，距今已经差不多二十年了。现在您的理论不光涉及语言教学，而且和公民教育也有关系。所以，我想了解

一下您怎么看待您自己的理论。您能不能评价一下自己的理论？谢谢。

Michael Byram：在1997年写了这本书之后，加入公民教育这个维度的想法对我来说就变得愈发清晰了。在2000年左右，我和大学的同事一起开了很多研讨会，也出版了关于公民教育的书籍。我的想法是把公民教育与外语教学结合起来，但不是所有人都认同这种立场。我并不是说你们应该要这么做，只是想给大家提供一种思路，让大家思考一下是否应在教学中加入社区行动这个维度。从这个意义上说，通过为语言教学加入新的维度，我希望自己比1997年写作那本书时有所进步。

当然对于我的模型也有一些批评意见。有些批评意见是好的，因为没有什么东西是完美的。也许我也应该强调一下，这个模型其实只是针对语言教学的，还有很多模型是出于不同的目的开发出来的。现在让我讲一讲对此问题稍微个人的看法作为总结。作为大学教授，我的工作之一就是审阅博士论文。我常常被邀去做外审，因为很多学生在论文中使用了我的理论。在大多情况下，我发现他们都没有批判地评论我的理论。所以在论文答辩时我问的第一个问题就是："你为什么不批判一下 Byram 的这个模型呢？"他们都说："我怎么可能批判你的模型"。而我给出的回答是："这就是你这篇论文的弱点。"你必须批判。万事都有改进的空间。从这个意义上说，我可以重写这本书，但我不会这么做。它会保持原样，交给后人去改进。

主持人：谢谢大家，Michael Byram 教授讲座的内容就到此结束了。大

with foreign language education. Not everybody would take that position. I am not here to say that you should, but it's something for you to think about, whether you add an action in the community dimension to what you are doing. In that sense, I hope I have improved from what I wrote in 1997 by adding a dimension to what language teaching should be.

There have been criticisms of my model. And there have been good criticisms. Nothing is perfect. Perhaps I should also emphasise that it is a model which is only for language teaching. There are dozens of models which are produced for different purposes. Let me tell you a little personal view on this now to finish with. One of my jobs as a professor is to examine PhD theses. I'm often invited to examine theses because the students have used my work. And in most cases, I find that they do not criticise my work. So the first question I asked them in the defence of their thesis was: Why don't you criticise Byram's model? They all sit back and say, 'Oh because I can't possibly criticise your model'. And my answer to that was, 'that is the weakness of your thesis'. You must criticise. Everything can be improved upon. In that sense, I could rewrite the book, but I won't rewrite the book. It will stand as it is and be improved by other people.

Host: I believe all have enjoyed so much for his talks. Let's join together to give him a warm applause for him to give us so great lectures in the past two days. Thank you very much. We should also thank Hanban for giving us the opportunity to get to know Professor Byram's work. I know you still have a lot of questions to discuss with him. But the good beginning is half done. So you have the chance. You still can contact Professor Byram through multiple media, emails or Facebook or whatever. (Byram: Not Facebook. I don't have Facebook.) You can continue this kind of discussion.

Michael Byram: Can I also say thank you? I would like to say thank you for your questions especially the difficult ones which I didn't answer. I know I didn't answer all the questions well. I try my best but I don't answer

家都从中受益良多。我们一起用热烈的掌声感谢 Michael Byram 教授，感谢他在两天时间里给我们做了这么精彩的讲座。同时我们也要感谢汉办给我们机会来了解 Byram 教授的理论和著作。我知道大家还有很多问题想和教授交流，但好的开始是成功的一半，大家以后还会有这样的机会。大家还可以通过多媒体、电子邮件或其他方式与教授联系，继续相关的讨论。

Michael Byram：我也非常感谢大家。感谢大家的提问，虽然有些问题我也很难给出回答。我知道其实我并没有回答好所有的问题。我尽力了，但有些问题还是没有回答好。我还想特别感谢翻译，他们为我和在座的各位提供了莫大的帮助。你们的工作非常出色，感谢你们的帮助。

them all well. But above all, I'd like to thank our interpreters who have done an excellent job for me and for many of you. You've done a wonderful job. Thank you very much.

参考文献
References

[1] Anderson, B. *Imagined Communities*. London: Verso, 1991.

[2] Bennett, M. Towards Ethnorelativism: A Developmental Model of Intercultural Sensitivity. In R. M. Paige (ed.) *Education for the Intercultural Experience*. 2nd edition. Intercultural Press, inc., 1993. http://www.library.wisc.edu/EDVRC/docs/public/pdfs/SEEDReadings/intCulSens.pdf

[3] Byram, M. *Teaching and Assessing Intercultural Communicative Competence*. Clevedon: Multilingual Matters, 1997.

[4] Byram, M. *From Foreign Language Education to Education for Intercultural Citizenship: Essays and Reflections*. Clevedon: Multilingual Matters, 2008.

[5] Byram, M., Conlon Perugini, D. and Wagner, M. The Development of Intercultural Citizenship in the Elementary School Spanish Classroom. *Learning Languages Contents*, 2013, 18(2): 16-31.

[6] Council of Europe. *Common European Framework of Reference for Languages: Teaching, Learning, Assessment*. Strasbourg: Council of Europe, 2001.

[7] Council of Europe. *Autobiography of Intercultural Encounters*. Strasbourg: Council of Europe, 2010. www.coe.int/lang-autobiography

[8] Council of Europe. *Competences for Democratic Culture*. Strasbourg: Council of Europe, 2016. https://book.coe.int/eur/en/human-rights-education-intercultural-education/6871-competencies-for-democratic-culture-living-together-as-equals-in-culturally-diverse-democratic-societies.html

[9] Fox, K. *Watching the English: The Hidden Rules of English Behaviour*. London: Hodder and Stoughton, 2004.

[10] Parsons, J. and Junge, P. Why Do Danes Put Their Elderly in Nursing Homes? Working Outside the Classroom with Adult Second Language Learners. In: Byram, M., Nichols, A. and Stevens, D. (eds.) *Developing Intercultural Competence in Practice*. Clevedon: Multilingual Matters, 2001.

[11] Porto, M. and Yulita, L. Language and Intercultural Citizenship Education for a Culture of Peace: The Case of the Malvinas/Falklands Project in Language Teaching in Higher Education. In: Byram, M. Golubeva, I. Han, H. and Wagner, M (eds.) *From Principles to Practice in Education for Intercultural Citizenship*. Bristol: Multilingual Matters, 2016.

[12] Porto, M., Daryai-Hansen, P., Arcuri, M. E. and Schifler, K. Green Kidz: Young Learners Engage in Intercultural Environmental Citizenship in English Language Classroom in Argentina and Denmark. In: Byram, M. Golubeva, I. Han, H. and Wagner, M (eds.) *From Principles to Practice in Education for Intercultural Citizenship*. Bristol: Multilingual Matters, 2016.

[13] Risager, K. *Language and Culture: Global Flows and Local Complexity*. Clevedon: Multilingual Matters, 2006.

[14] Ryle, G. Knowing How and Knowing That: The Presidential Address. *Proceedings of the Aristotelian Society*, 1945, 46:1–16.

[15] Street, B. Culture Is a Verb: Anthropological Aspects of Language and Cultural Process. In D. Graddol, M. Byram L. and Thompson (eds.). *Language and Culture*. Clevedon: Multilingual Matters, 1993.

[16] Trim, J. L. M. The Common European Framework of Reference for Languages and Its Background: A Case Study of Cultural Politics and Educational Influences. In: Byram, M. and Parmenter, L. (eds.) *The Common European Framework of Reference: The Globalisation of Language Education Policy*. Bristol: Multilingual Matters, 2012.

[17] Topuzova, K. British and Bulgarian Christmas Cards: A Research Project for Students. In: Byram, M., Nichols, A. and Stevens, D. 2001, *Developing Intercultural Competence in Practice*. Clevedon: Multilingual Matters, 2001.